Careers in Focus

Careers in Focus

COMPUTERS

FIFTH EDITION

Ferguson
An imprint of Infobase Publishing

Careers in Focus: Computers, Fifth Edition

Copyright © 2008 by Infobase Publishing

Ferguson
An imprint of Infobase Publishing
132 West 31st Street
New York NY 10001

Library of Congress Cataloging-in-Publication Data

Careers in focus : computers. — 5th ed.
    p. cm.
  Includes bibliographical references and index.
  ISBN-13: 978-0-8160-7285-9 (alk. paper)
  ISBN-10: 0-8160-7285-X (alk. paper)
    1. Computer science—Vocational guidance—Juvenile literature. I. Title:
Computers.
  QA76.25.C295 2008
  004.023—dc22
                                2008028244

Ferguson books are available at special discounts when purchased in bulk quantities for businesses, associations, institutions, or sales promotions. Please call our Special Sales Department in New York at (212) 967-8800 or (800) 322-8755.

You can find Ferguson on the World Wide Web at http://www.fergpubco.com

Text design by David Strelecky
Cover design by Salvatore Luongo

Printed in the United States of America

MP MSRF 10 9 8 7 6 5 4 3 2

This book is printed on acid-free paper.

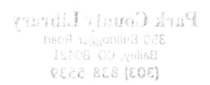

Table of Contents

Introduction

The computer industry offers a wide range of rewarding careers. Many positions overlap and not every company hires people in each functional area. These basic areas are design, programming, administration, and service.

For our purposes, *designers* include researchers who evaluate the market or existing technology to find opportunities for improvements or new product design. Researchers have considerable freedom to explore uncharted areas of computer technology. Often their ideas are not implemented for years, until the market catches up to the theory.

Designers usually work on a project that has already been defined in some way. For example, a company's accounting department might request a special system to improve its operations. A software designer is assigned to handle that problem. Generally, designers use their knowledge of hardware and software to design a computer system and set of applications that will solve a business or scientific problem. More specifically, designers can specialize in databases, networks, or software applications.

Computers, regardless of function, are based on the principles and processes of mathematics. The basic design process is similar regardless of job title: The problem is defined, equipment is analyzed and upgraded if need be, software is customized, and new programming fills any gaps.

Programming is much more detail-oriented and less abstract than design analysis. It can involve hardware, software, or both. In any case, programmers write the coded instructions that make computers do what we want them to do. *Systems programmers* write the instructions that make different computers and peripherals perform well together. *Software programmers* write instructions for how computers should respond to various input and what on-screen displays should be generated. Programmers are required to know at least one, but usually more, computer programming language, including BASIC, COBOL, FORTRAN, RPG, CSP, C++, and Java.

Computer administrators are in charge of daily operations of different kinds of computer systems. The most common areas of specialization are database, network, systems security, and quality assurance. Administrators are responsible for a variety of tasks. They help install new systems, train new users, and address user problems as they arise. Administrators are also involved with backing up the system regularly. They also ensure good systems communications. If a network server goes down, for example, a network administrator attempts to isolate the cause of the problem and fix it. If it is too complicated, the administrator must call in higher-level systems people.

Computer service is another broad category of careers in the computer industry. *Systems setup specialists, computer support specialists,* and *computer repairer technicians* are included in this group. Systems setup specialists install new hardware and software either at the client site or in a service center (in the case of software). Large installations at major corporations can take days or even weeks to install properly. Setup work requires solid knowledge in the basics of computer technology as well as strong manual dexterity. Sometimes systems are so complicated that specialists are called to help plan the layout of the computer room, both of the multitude of wires and the physical equipment.

Computer support specialists can also specialize in either hardware or software. They work in large corporations or for computer companies that offer technical support to end users. For example, a large bank probably has a computer support person on staff in the information systems department. This individual is responsible for helping users when they encounter problems and for fixing problems with the machines when they break down or crash. Support specialists who work for a computer manufacturer may answer phone calls from frustrated users who cannot get their computers or applications to run properly. These specialists talk consumers through the problems and attempt to solve them over the phone.

Computer repairer technicians are called in when the hardware breaks down physically. Transistors can blow, for example, or systems boards or other internal hardware can be defective from the start. Computer repairer technicians analyze the hardware, determine the cause of the problem, and fix it by repairing the equipment or replacing certain parts with new ones.

As the Internet continues to change the way we live and work, job titles and descriptions are defined almost daily and change rapidly. There are, however, a few positions that seem to be constant. *Internet/intranet technology managers* oversee programmers and designers who work on both the Internet and intranets (networks within various companies). These managers prioritize strategies to accomplish specific goals, distribute budgets, write proposals concerning the best use of the company's technological resources, and oversee the development and implementation of company strategic plans. *Webmasters* are accountable for making sure that the site works correctly. They maintain, augment, and improve the site, as well as check for consistency and install tools for updating site content. *Web designers* (and sometimes *Web editors*) develop the look, layout, and overall impact of the site. They must incorporate information gathered from copywriters and marketing managers into functional, intriguing, and user-friendly designs.

Many different types of companies hire computer professionals. Computer manufacturers and software companies hire the whole range of professionals. Many of these employers are clustered in certain geographical areas, like northern California, Seattle, and parts of the East Coast. Living in an area with many potential employers increases the likelihood of being hired (or rehired) by an employer relatively quickly.

Computer companies range from huge market leaders to small start-ups. In addition, there are thousands of small- to medium-sized companies that create specialized products, such as software to be used specifically to run corporate human resources departments. Start-ups are generally considered to be a risky investment until a major player, such as Microsoft, shows interest in them by buying stock. If that happens, the start-up owners can become instant millionaires.

Large corporations are major employers of computer professionals as well. Many maintain information systems (IS) departments, which hire people for the many different positions described earlier. The number of in-house information systems departments has grown with the increased usage of computers in the workplace. Almost all companies, including banks, insurance companies, consumer products firms, and government agencies, have IS departments.

Other employers of computer professionals are consulting firms, such as Accenture, Deloitte & Touche, and McKinsey & Company. They hire college graduates with degrees in computer science to help them integrate the latest technology into their clients' business. Most of these jobs are based in large cities and require a lot of travel.

Employment for most computer professionals is expected to be strong as technology becomes more sophisticated and organizations continue to adopt and integrate these technologies, making for plentiful job openings. Falling prices of computer hardware and software should continue to induce more businesses to expand computerized operations and integrate new technologies. To maintain a competitive edge and operate more cost-effectively, firms will continue to demand computer professionals who are knowledgeable about the latest technologies and are able to apply them to the needs of business.

As for the Internet, the expanding integration of Internet technologies has resulted in a rising demand for a variety of skilled professionals who can develop and support Internet, Intranet, and World

Wide Web applications. Growth in these areas is also expected to create demand for computer scientists, database administrators, engineers, and systems analysts who are knowledgeable about networks, databases, and communications security.

Employment opportunities in the computer industry are numerous and varied. Flexibility is also key because as the industry shifts into new, unexplored areas, computer professionals have to shift as well. In addition, many computer professionals use certain jobs as springboards to other higher-level jobs. For example, few professionals want to work in computer support long-term, but many start there to get a foot in the door before internal positions open up.

According to the U.S. Department of Labor, employment of programmers should grow more slowly than the average for all occupations as a result of the emergence of new technologies that eliminate the need for some routine programming work of the past, the outsourcing of programming jobs overseas, the increased availability of packaged software programs, and the increased sophistication of computer users who are able to write and implement their own programs. Employment of computer and peripheral equipment operators is expected to grow more slowly than the rest of the industry. As automation continues to increase productivity, automated systems and robotic equipment should reduce the need for such workers. Opportunities in computer and electronic product manufacturing are expected to decline over the next decade.

Three things are essential to aspiring computer professionals: determination to keep up with the latest technology, flexibility, and formal education. Of course, a solid understanding of computer basics is required as well. However, the technology of today will be obsolete in months, if not weeks, and only those individuals who strive to be on the cutting edge will have long-term growth potential during their careers.

Each article in *Careers in Focus: Computers* discusses a particular computer occupation in detail. The articles appear in Ferguson's *Encyclopedia of Careers and Vocational Guidance* but have been updated and revised with the latest information from the U.S. Department of Labor and other sources.

The following paragraphs detail the sections and features that appear in the book.

The **Quick Facts** section provides a brief summary of the career including recommended school subjects, personal skills, work environment, minimum educational requirements, salary ranges, certification or licensing requirements, and employment outlook. This section also provides acronyms and identification numbers for the following government classification indexes: the *Dictionary of Occupational Titles* (DOT), the *Guide for Occupational Exploration* (GOE), the National Occupational Classification (NOC) Index, and the Occupational Information Network (O*NET)-Standard Occupational Classification System (SOC) index. The DOT, GOE, and O*NET-SOC indexes have been created by the U.S. government; the NOC index is Canada's career classification system. Readers can use the identification numbers listed in the Quick Facts section to access further information about a career. Print editions of the DOT (*Dictionary of Occupational Titles*. Indianapolis, Ind.: JIST Works, 1991) and GOE (*Guide for Occupational Exploration*. Indianapolis, Ind.: JIST Works, 2001) are available at libraries. Electronic versions of the NOC (http:// www23.hrdc-drhc.gc.ca) and O*NET-SOC (http://online.onetcenter. org) are available on the Internet. When no DOT, GOE, NOC, or O*NET-SOC numbers are present, this means that the U.S. Department of Labor or Human Resources Development Canada have not created a numerical designation for this career. In this instance, you will see the acronym "N/A," or not available.

The **Overview** section is a brief introductory description of the duties and responsibilities involved in this career. Oftentimes, a career may have a variety of job titles. When this is the case, alternative career titles are presented. Employment statistics are also provided, when available.

The **History** section describes the history of the particular job as it relates to the overall development of its industry or field.

The Job describes the primary and secondary duties of the job.

Requirements discusses high school and postsecondary education and training requirements, any certification or licensing that is necessary, and other personal requirements for success in the job.

Exploring offers suggestions on how to gain experience in or knowledge of the particular job before making a firm educational and financial commitment. The focus is on what can be done while still in high school (or in the early years of college) to gain a better understanding of the job.

The **Employers** section gives an overview of typical places of employment for the job.

Starting Out discusses the best ways to land that first job, be it through the college career services office, newspaper ads, Internet employment sites, or personal contact.

The **Advancement** section describes what kind of career path to expect from the job and how to get there.

Earnings lists salary ranges and describes the typical fringe benefits.

The **Work Environment** section describes the typical surroundings and conditions of employment—whether indoors or outdoors, noisy or quiet, social or independent. Also discussed are typical hours worked, any seasonal fluctuations, and the stresses and strains of the job.

The **Outlook** section summarizes the job in terms of the general economy and industry projections. For the most part, Outlook information is obtained from the U.S. Bureau of Labor Statistics and is supplemented by information gathered from professional associations. Job growth terms follow those used in the *Occupational Outlook Handbook*. Growth described as "much faster than the average" means an increase of 27 percent or more. Growth described as "faster than the average" means an increase of 18 to 26 percent. Growth described as "about as fast as the average" means an increase of 9 to 17 percent. Growth described as "more slowly than the average" means an increase of 0 to 8 percent. "Decline" means a decrease by any amount.

Each article ends with **For More Information,** which lists organizations that provide information on training, education, internships, scholarships, and job placement.

Throughout the book you will also find informative sidebars, photos of some of the careers, and interviews with professionals working in the computer field.

If you have an avid interest in computing and enjoy problem solving, one of the careers in this book might be a good choice for you. Read the articles and discuss your interests with parents, teachers, and friends. Also, continue to use and explore computers in your free time. Any experience you gain now can give you an advantage in this competitive and challenging field.

College Professors, Computer Science

OVERVIEW

Computer science professors instruct undergraduate and graduate students in the subject of computer science at colleges and universities. They are responsible for lecturing classes, leading small seminar groups, and creating and grading examinations. They also may conduct research, write for publication, and aid in administration. There are approximately 45,000 computer science teachers at the postsecondary level.

HISTORY

The concept of colleges and universities goes back many centuries. These institutions evolved slowly from monastery schools, which trained a select few for certain professions, notably theology. The terms *college* and *university* have become virtually interchangeable in America outside the walls of academia, although originally they designated two very different kinds of institutions.

Two of the most notable early European universities were the University of Bologna in Italy, thought to have been established in the 12th century, and the University of Paris, which was chartered in 1201. These universities were considered models after which other European universities were patterned. Oxford University in England was probably established during the 12th century. Oxford served as a model for early American colleges and universities and today is still considered one of the world's leading institutions.

Harvard, the first U.S. college, was established in 1636. Its stated purpose was to train men for the ministry; the early colleges were all

QUICK FACTS

School Subjects
Computers
English
Speech

Personal Skills
Communication/ideas
Helping/teaching

Work Environment
Primarily indoors
Primarily one location

Minimum Education Level
Master's degree

Salary Range
$32,130 to $57,620 to $108,780+

Certification or Licensing
None available

Outlook
Much faster than the average

DOT
090

GOE
12.03.02

NOC
4121

O*NET-SOC
25-1021.00

established for religious training. With the growth of state-supported institutions in the early 18th century, the process of freeing the curriculum from ties with the church began. The University of Virginia established the first liberal arts curriculum in 1825, and these innovations were later adopted by many other colleges and universities.

Although the original colleges in the United States were patterned after Oxford University, they later came under the influence of German universities. During the 19th century, more than nine thousand Americans went to Germany to study. The emphasis in German universities was on the scientific method. Most of the people who had studied in Germany returned to the United States to teach in universities, bringing this objective, factual approach to education and to other fields of learning.

In 1833, Oberlin College in Oberlin, Ohio, became the first college founded as a coeducational institution. In 1836, the first women-only college, Wesleyan Female College, was founded in Macon, Georgia.

The junior college movement in the United States has been one of the most rapidly growing educational developments. Junior colleges first came into being just after the turn of the 20th century.

The first computer science program was founded at Harvard University. Today, nearly every college and university in the United States offers computer science or information technology–related majors.

THE JOB

Computer science faculty members teach at junior colleges or at four-year colleges and universities. At four-year institutions, most faculty members are *assistant professors, associate professors,* or *full professors.* These three types of professorships differ in regards to status, job responsibilities, and salary. Assistant professors are new faculty members who are working to get tenure (status as a permanent professor); they seek to advance to associate and then to full professorships.

Computer science professors perform three main functions: teaching, advising, and research. Their most important responsibility is to teach students. Their role within the department will determine the level of courses they teach and the number of courses per semester. Most professors work with students at all levels, from college freshmen to graduate students. They may head several classes a semester or only a few a year. Some of their classes will have large enrollment, while graduate seminars may consist of only 12 or fewer students. Though professors may spend fewer than 10 hours a week in the actual classroom, they spend many hours preparing lectures and lesson plans, grading papers and exams, and preparing grade reports.

A computer science professor (standing) observes students during a class. *(Don Ryan, AP Images)*

They also schedule office hours during the week to be available to students outside of the lecture hall, and they meet with students individually throughout the semester. In the classroom, professors lecture, lead discussions, administer exams, and assign textbook reading and other research. While most professors teach entry-level computer science classes such as "Introduction to Computer Science" or "Foundations of Computer Science," some also teach higher-level classes that center on a particular specialty. For a computer graphics class, for example, professors may teach students how to create computerized animation, digital illustration, or web design. Professors teaching software engineering classes may specialize in software design and development or information systems. In some courses, they rely heavily on computer laboratories to teach course material.

Another important responsibility is advising students. Not all faculty members serve as advisers, but those who do must set aside large blocks of time to guide students through the program. College professors who serve as advisers may have any number of students assigned to them, from fewer than 10 to more than 100, depending on the administrative policies of the college. Their responsibility may involve looking over a planned program of studies to make sure the students meet requirements for graduation, or it may involve working intensively with each student on many aspects of college life. They may also discuss the different fields of computer science with students and help them identify the best career choices.

The third responsibility of college and university faculty members is research and publication. Faculty members who are heavily involved in research programs sometimes are assigned a smaller teaching load. College computer science professors publish their research findings in various scholarly journals such as the *Journal on Emerging Technologies in Computing Systems* and *Computing in Science & Engineering*. They also write books based on their research or on their own knowledge and experience in the field. Most textbooks are written by college and university teachers, or veterans of the computer industry. Publishing a significant amount of work has been the traditional standard by which assistant professors prove themselves worthy of becoming permanent, tenured faculty. Typically, pressure to publish is greatest for assistant professors. Pressure to publish increases again if an associate professor wishes to be considered for a promotion to full professorship.

In recent years, some liberal arts colleges have recognized that the pressure to publish is taking faculty away from their primary duties to the students, and these institutions have begun to place a decreasing emphasis on publishing and more on performance in the classroom. Professors in junior colleges face less pressure to publish than those in four-year institutions.

Some faculty members eventually rise to the position of *department chair*, where they govern the affairs of an entire computer science department. Department chairs, faculty, and other professional staff members are aided in their myriad duties by *graduate assistants*, who may help develop teaching materials, moderate computer laboratories, conduct research, give examinations, teach lower-level courses, and carry out other activities.

Some computer science professors may also conduct classes in an extension program. In such a program, they teach evening and weekend courses for the benefit of people who otherwise would not be able to take advantage of the institution's resources. They may travel away from the campus and meet with a group of students at another location. They may work full time for the extension division or may divide their time between on-campus and off-campus teaching.

Distance learning programs, an increasingly popular option for students, give professors the opportunity to use today's technologies to remain in one place while teaching students who are at a variety of locations simultaneously. The professor's duties, like those when teaching correspondence courses conducted by mail, include grading work that students send in at periodic intervals and advising students of their progress. Computers, the Internet, email, and video conferencing, however, are some of the technology tools that allow professors and students to communicate in "real time" in a virtual classroom setting. Meetings may be scheduled during the same time as traditional classes or during evenings and weekends. Professors who do this work are sometimes known as *extension work, correspondence,* or *distance learning instructors.* They may teach online courses in addition to other classes or may have distance learning as their major teaching responsibility.

The *junior college instructor* has many of the same kinds of responsibilities as does the teacher in a four-year college or university. Because junior colleges offer only a two-year program, they teach only undergraduates.

REQUIREMENTS

High School

Your high school's college preparatory program likely includes courses in computers (take as many as you can), English, science, foreign language, history, and mathematics. In addition, you should take courses in speech to get a sense of what it will be like to lecture to a group of students. Your school's debate team can also help you develop public speaking skills, along with research skills.

Postsecondary Training

At least one advanced degree in computer science, computer engineering, information management, Information Technology, or another computer field is required to be a professor in a college or university. The master's degree is the minimum standard, and graduate work beyond the master's is usually desirable. If you hope to advance in academic rank above instructor, most institutions require a doctorate. Many large universities and colleges have a strong preference for those with a Ph.D. in computer science, information management, or a closely related field.

In the last year of your undergraduate program, you'll apply to graduate programs in your area of study. Standards for admission to a graduate program can be high and the competition heavy, depending on the school. Once accepted into a program, your responsibilities will be similar to those of your professors—in addition to attending seminars, you'll research, prepare articles for publication, and teach some undergraduate courses.

You may find employment in a junior college with only a master's degree. Advancement in responsibility and in salary, however, is more likely to come if you have earned a doctorate.

Other Requirements

You should definitely like working with computers, but also enjoy reading, writing, and researching. Not only will you spend many years studying in school, but your whole career will be based on communicating your thoughts and ideas, as well as abstract concepts to students. People skills are important because you'll be dealing directly with students, administrators, and other faculty members on a daily basis. You should feel comfortable in a role of authority and possess self-confidence.

EXPLORING

Learn as much as you can about computer hardware, computer software, and the Internet. Visit Web sites and read books and magazines that relate to computers.

Your high school computer science teachers use many of the same skills as college computer science professors, so talk to your teachers about their careers and their college experiences. You can develop your own teaching experience by volunteering at a community center, working at a day care center, or working at a summer camp. Also, spend some time on a college campus to get a sense of the environment. Write to colleges for their admissions brochures and course catalogs (or check them out online); read about the faculty members and the courses they teach. Before visiting college campuses, make arrangements to speak to professors who teach courses that interest you. These professors may allow you to sit in on their classes or labs and observe. Also, make appointments with college advisers and with people in the admissions and recruitment offices. If your grades are good enough, you might be able to serve as a teaching assistant during your undergraduate years, which can give you experience leading discussions and grading papers.

EMPLOYERS

Approximately 45,000 computer science faculty are employed in the United States. Employment opportunities vary based on area of study and education. Most universities have many different departments that hire faculty. With a doctorate, a number of publications, and a record of good teaching, professors should find opportunities in universities all across the country. Professors teach in undergraduate and graduate programs. The teaching jobs at doctoral institutions are usually better paying and more prestigious. The most sought-after positions are those that offer tenure. Teachers who have only a master's degree will be limited to opportunities with junior colleges, community colleges, and some small private institutions.

STARTING OUT

You should start the process of finding a teaching position while you are in graduate school. The process includes developing a curriculum vitae (a detailed, academic resume), writing for publication, assisting with research, attending conferences, and gaining teaching experience and recommendations. Many students begin applying for teaching positions while finishing their graduate program. For most positions at four-year institutions, you must travel to large conferences where interviews can be arranged with representatives from the universities to which you have applied.

Because of the competition for tenure-track positions, you may have to work for a few years in temporary positions, visiting various schools as an *adjunct professor*. Some professional associations maintain lists of teaching opportunities in their areas. They may also make lists of applicants available to college administrators looking to fill an available position.

Some professors begin teaching after having successful careers in the computer industry.

ADVANCEMENT

The normal pattern of advancement is from instructor to assistant professor, to associate professor, to full professor. All four academic ranks are concerned primarily with teaching and research. College faculty members who have an interest in and a talent for administration may be advanced to department chair or dean of their college. A few become college or university presidents or other types of administrators.

The instructor is usually an inexperienced college teacher. He or she may hold a doctorate or may have completed all the Ph.D. requirements except for the dissertation. Most colleges look upon the rank of instructor as the period during which the college is trying out the teacher. Instructors usually are advanced to the position of assistant professors within three to four years. Assistant professors are given up to about six years to prove themselves worthy of tenure, and if they do so, they become associate professors. Some professors choose to remain at the associate level. Others strive to become full professors and receive greater status, salary, and responsibilities.

Most colleges have clearly defined promotion policies from rank to rank for faculty members, and many have written statements about the number of years in which instructors and assistant professors may remain in grade. Administrators in many colleges hope to encourage younger faculty members to increase their skills and competencies and thus to qualify for the more responsible positions of associate professor and full professor.

EARNINGS

According to the U.S. Department of Labor, in 2006, the median salary for all computer science postsecondary instructors was $57,620, with 10 percent earning $108,780 or more and 10 percent earning $32,130 or less. Those with the highest earnings tend to be senior tenured faculty; those with the lowest, graduate assistants. Professors working on the West Coast and the East Coast and those working at doctorate-granting institutions also tend to earn the highest salaries. Many professors try to increase their earnings by completing research, publishing in their field, or teaching additional courses.

Benefits for full-time faculty typically include health insurance and retirement funds and, in some cases, stipends for travel related to research, housing allowances, and tuition waivers for dependents.

WORK ENVIRONMENT

A college or university is usually a pleasant place in which to work. Campuses bustle with all types of activities and events, stimulating ideas, and a young, energetic population. Much prestige comes with success as a professor and scholar; professors have the respect of students, colleagues, and others in their community.

Depending on the size of the department, computer science professors may have their own office, or they may have to share an office with one or more colleagues. Their department may provide them with a computer, Internet access, and research assistants. College professors are also able to do much of their office work at home. They can arrange their schedule around class hours, academic meetings, and the established office hours when they meet with students. Most computer science teachers work more than 40 hours each week. Although computer science teachers may teach only two or three classes a semester, they spend many hours preparing for lectures, examining student work, and conducting research.

OUTLOOK

The U.S. Department of Labor predicts much faster than average employment growth for college and university professors through 2014. College enrollment is projected to grow due to an increased number of 18- to 24-year-olds, an increased number of adults returning to college, and an increased number of foreign-born students. Retirement of current faculty members will also provide job openings. However, competition for full-time, tenure-track positions at four-year schools will be very strong.

FOR MORE INFORMATION

To read about the issues affecting college professors, contact the following organizations:

American Association of University Professors
1012 14th Street, NW, Suite 500
Washington, DC 20005-3406
Tel: 202-737-5900
Email: aaup@aaup.org
http://www.aaup.org

American Federation of Teachers
555 New Jersey Avenue, NW
Washington, DC 20001-2029
Tel: 202-879-4400
Email: online@aft.org
http://www.aft.org

For information on internships, student membership, and the student magazine, Crossroads, *contact*
Association for Computing Machinery
1515 Broadway
New York, NY 10036-8901
Tel: 212-869-7440
http://www.acm.org

For information on scholarships, student membership, and to read Careers in Computer Science and Computer Engineering, *visit the IEEE's Web site:*

IEEE Computer Society
1730 Massachusetts Avenue, NW
Washington, DC 20036-1992
Tel: 202-371-0101
http://www.computer.org

——— INTERVIEW ———

Dr. Matthew Jaffe is an associate professor of computer science and the chair of the Computer Science Program at Embry-Riddle Aeronautical University (ERAU) in Prescott, Arizona. He discussed the field with the editors of Careers in Focus: Computers.

Q. Please tell us about your professional background.

A. I started academic life intending to be a mathematician and so studied mathematics as an undergraduate at the University of California, Berkeley, after which the U.S. Navy sent me to graduate school to study Aeronautical Systems at the University of West Florida. Subsequently, I become a naval tactical data systems officer and developed extensive operational experience with the real-time, human-machine decision making systems that remain fascinating to me to this day. After leaving active duty with the navy, I went to work as a software/systems engineer in the aerospace industry, working on ever more complex human-machine systems. After several years of spending most of my lunch hours studying on my own in the company library, I decided I should try to get some academic credit for the hours I was putting in. When I came up for air, I had a Ph.D. in information and computer sciences from the University of California, Irvine. I continued to work in the aerospace industry until both my children graduated from college, at which point I could afford the substantial salary cut entailed in becoming the academic I always wanted to be. At that point, I moved here to Embry-Riddle Aeronautical University/Prescott where I have been a program or department chair of computer science, computer engineering, and/or software engineering since 1996.

Q. Tell us about your program.

A. ERAU/Prescott offers two related degrees that share a common core of educational objectives: Computer Science, for those students whose interests lie more in the software domain than with hardware, and Computer Engineering, for those more interested in digital hardware design than with software. But there is, by intention, a large degree of overlap between the two programs. In order to be able to predict and optimize the behavior of the software that they design, computer scientists and software engineers need a good understanding of the hardware on which their software will run; while hardware engineers need to understand the different needs of the different types of software that their hardware will host.

In addition to acquiring a broad set of core competencies in computer science (as well as the mathematics, natural sciences, social sciences, and humanities required for any baccalaureate degree), computer science students here must select a track of specialization for more detailed study. We have pre-defined tracks in Space Physics, Business, Defense Systems, and Global Security and Intelligence; but students are encouraged to propose customized tracks tailored to match their specific interests. The recent increased interest on the part of both students, potential employers, and faculty in information and computer security has led us to develop more courses in these areas in recent years, and we are considering offering a new degree in that area in the fairly near future.

In addition to the full Computer Science major itself, we offer three minors for students from other majors: Computer Science, Computer Security, and Computer Applications. The first two should be pretty self-explanatory; the third, computer applications, is oriented towards students with an interest in commercial and business data processing. In addition, ERAU/ Prescott supports what we call a "designer minor" if one of the three predefined ones isn't a good enough match for a student's interests.

Q. What types of internships are available to students at your school?

A. Both the Computer Science (CS) faculty and our career counseling staff maintain pretty extensive ties with industry so we can offer a pretty diverse set of internships all over the country. There are a large number of companies and research centers that particularly value Embry-Riddle CS students and are eager to get an early look at them. In the last few years we have had our students intern at various NASA facilities [including the Dryden Flight Research Center, the Jet Propulsion Laboratory (JPL), and NASA Langley Research Center], the Mitre Corporation (a federal research center specializing in computer security, among many other things), Raytheon, Honeywell, Airborne Communications and Surveillance Systems, and Sierra Nevada Corporation. My sister is a principal engineer at NASA JPL specializing in deep space telemetry and I have once or twice, and only for my very best students, asked her to supervise them herself and personally sweat them hard for the summer. The students, of course, loved it and JPL thought so highly of one of them that it almost refused to send him back to us.

Although a real world summer internship is not a requirement for graduation, we strongly encourage our students to consider one. It's obviously a win-win situation—our students get paid to get invaluable real-world experience that often leads them to appreciate their required coursework here all the more while the companies and research centers get a chance to impress the students and so hope to gain an edge hiring them after they graduate.

Q. What is one thing that young people may not know about a career in computer science?

A. How diverse it can be. First there's the obvious diversity of application area: Software is an intensely protean technology and is central to businesses across the board and to avionics, security systems, air traffic management, airport operations, animation, gaming, medical equipment, communications systems, and so on almost ad infinitum. Modern computer scientists may work in software systems requirements development, which requires them to pick up a fair bit of domain knowledge in whichever domain(s) their company or research center is focused on, software architectural design and analysis, programming itself, software test and integration (and the extensive planning that precedes it), or software installation at customer sites around the world. Some engineers like to do them all, some like to specialize in one area and stay there their entire career. Many of the larger aerospace companies, by the way, aware that most new CS graduates do not realize the full range of professional activities available to them, have what they call "rotator" programs where a new graduate can work for several months in each area before picking one to focus on for the first few years of professional development.

Q. What types of students pursue study in your program?

A. That's not as easy a question to answer is it was to ask; students in computer science tend to be a pretty diverse lot; so I think I'll pick just one or two characteristics that I think I see fairly often in our students.

To begin with, I think most of them share a bit of genuine intellectual curiosity, however shy they might be at the beginning about letting their professors see it. They tend to be a little brighter than the average, and I think they hope that their college professors will expose them to genuine wisdom. They have a vague but hopeful image of a university as a place of wisdom but they fear being disappointed as they perhaps all too often were in their earlier schooling. So they're curious and hopeful, but cautious lest they be disappointed again. I'm sure that many other students, outside of computer science, share these traits, but it's my impression that it's pretty widespread in our CS students.

In terms of their academic interests, they, our CS students, obviously will be more technophilic than most and more oriented towards pragmatics than the abstract knowledge of the pure scientist. Computer science may attract them because they sense, correctly, that it offers a pretty nice blend of esthetically gorgeous theory with tremendously practical applications, much more so than many other engineering disciplines, in my personal opinion.

As a digression at this point (to amplify a bit on my use of the word "wisdom" earlier), I must note that although I don't think that we, as college professors (computer science or otherwise), are much wiser than other people, we *do* tend to at least have a lot of knowledge, however arcane, and often a passionate curiosity and I think that that combination winds up satisfying our students' hopes for exposure to wisdom. They *say*, when we interview them after graduation, that they are well satisfied with us, at any rate; and that's fortunate for us (their faculty): True wisdom is pretty rare; extensive technical knowledge and enthusiasm is about the most I personally aspire to and I would be very unhappy to think that despite it all, I still left my students disappointed.

Q. What advice would you give computer science majors as they graduate and look for jobs?

A. Well, here at Embry-Riddle, I'd strongly recommend that they come talk to me about it. By the time they're seniors, I've gotten to know all my students personally and know their strengths and weaknesses and can call my contacts at firms that I think will be a good match. (As a result of both the consulting work I do and the international avionics standardization committee [RTCA SC205/EUROCAE WG71] I serve on, I have friends [including former students] in every major aerospace and avionics company in North America and Europe.) Our career counseling and placement office, although not as personal about it as I am, can cast an even wider net, maintaining contacts even outside the aerospace domain that I personally am most familiar with.

If the intent of this question was to be more general and less to allow me to promote my own university (which I obviously like to do), here are two general tips:

Do a bit of research on a company before interviewing with them. The Web, of course, is wonderful for this. You don't need to memorize their profit and loss statements from the last 10 years, just learn a bit about what they do and what they think they are (corporate mission statements, although usually pretty fluffy, can nonetheless provide some general insight here). When I was a manager in industry, I used to interview a lot of new grads. Anyone who had taken the trouble to learn a bit about my company before an interview gained points in my book.

Make it a point to ask questions during an interview (and not just about salary). An interview is a two-way street; both sides are attempting to determine how good a match they are for each other. Do you want to go on to grad school at some point? Ask how interested the company is in supporting that (most, of course, will be very supportive but there are surprising exceptions). Does the notion of a rotator program, as I mentioned earlier, appeal to you? Ask if the company has such a program. If interviewees did not have questions for me during an interview, I would be very concerned about their intellectual curiosity in general and their level of interest in my company in specific.

Q. What computer science fields offer the best employment prospects?

A. Computer security, beyond any doubt; firms and agencies are pleading with us to get them more students in this area, particularly computer forensics. But don't think that to get a good job you have to squeeze into the latest niche even if it doesn't really interest you. The job market for computer science is hot across the boards. Almost every major aerospace firm is short of software talent. Various statistical analyses produced by both the government and the private sector continue to forecast a shortfall between the rate schools are graduating students with degrees in the computer sciences and the growing needs of industry. Remember, as I noted earlier, software is far and away the most protean of technologies; it is already central to almost every other technology around and it will become more so, not less so, as computing becomes more and more ubiquitous in our daily lives. The need for well-educated computer scientists and engineers with a broader perspective than just code slinging is going to continue to grow for the foreseeable future.

Computer and Office Machine Service Technicians

OVERVIEW

Computer and office machine service technicians install, calibrate, maintain, troubleshoot, and repair equipment such as computers and their peripherals, office equipment, and specialized electronic equipment used in many factories, hospitals, airplanes, and numerous other businesses. Computer and office machine service technicians, including those who work on automated teller machines, hold approximately 168,000 jobs in the United States.

HISTORY

When computers were introduced to the business world, businesses found their size to be cumbersome and their capabilities limited. Today, technological advances have made computers smaller yet more powerful in their speed and capabilities. As more businesses rely on computers and other office machines to help manage daily activities, access information, and link offices and resources, the need for experienced professionals to work and service these machines will increase. Service technicians are employed by many corporations, hospitals, and the government, as part of a permanent staff, or they may be contracted to work for other businesses.

THE JOB

L-3 Communications manufactures computer systems for a diverse group of clients such as Shell Oil, United Airlines, and the Chicago Board of Trade. Besides computer systems, they also offer services such as equipment maintenance contracts and customer training. Joey Arca, a service technician for L-3 Communications, loves the challenge and diversity of his job. He and other members of the staff are responsible for the installation of computer mainframes and systems, as well as training employees on the equipment. A large part of their work is the maintenance, diagnosis, and repair of computer equipment. Since the clients are located throughout the United States, Arca must often travel to different cities in his assigned district. He also presents company products and services to potential clients and bids for maintenance contracts.

"I don't always have to be at the office, which gives me a lot of freedom," says Arca. "Sometimes I call in from my home and get my scheduled appointments for the day." The freedom of not being deskbound does have its downfalls. "One of the most difficult parts of the job is not knowing when a computer will fail. I carry a pager 24/7, and if I get called, I'm bound to a two-hour response time."

Many times work is scheduled before or after regular working hours or on the weekend, because it's important to have the least amount of workday disruption. Arca is successful in his job because he keeps on top of technology that is constantly changing with continuing education classes and training seminars. He is also well versed in both hardware and software, especially system software.

High school students learn how to troubleshoot and repair computers. *(Bob Daemmrich, The Image Works)*

REQUIREMENTS

High School

Traditional high school courses such as mathematics, physical sciences, and other laboratory-based sciences can provide a strong foundation for understanding basic mechanical and electronics principles. English and speech classes can help boost your written and verbal communications skills. Shop classes dealing with electricity, electronics, and blueprint reading are also beneficial. Computer science classes, of course, will provide you with great experience with computer hardware and software.

Postsecondary Training

You may be able to find work with a high school diploma if you have a lot of practical, hands-on experience in the field. Usually, however, employers require job candidates to have at least an associate's degree in electronics. Joey Arca holds a bachelor of science degree in electrical engineering. He credits specialized classes such as Voice and Data Communications, Microprocessor Controls, and Digital Circuits as giving him a good base for his current work environment.

Certification or Licensing

Most employers require certification, though standards vary depending on the company. However many consider certification as a measure of industry knowledge. Certification can also give you a competitive edge when interviewing for a new job or negotiating for a higher salary.

A variety of certification programs are available from the International Society of Certified Electronics Technicians, the Institute for Certification of Computing Professionals, CompTIA: The Computing Technology Industry Association, and the Electronics Technicians Association International, among other organizations. After the successful completion of study and examination, you may be certified in fields such as computer, industrial, and electronic equipment. Continuing education credits are required for recertification, usually every two to four years. Arca is certified as a computer technician from the Association of Energy Engineers and the Electronics Technicians Association International.

Other Requirements

A strong technical background and an aptitude for learning about new technologies, good communications skills, and superior manual dexterity will help you succeed in this industry. You'll also need to be motivated to keep up with modern computer and office machine technology. Machines rapidly become obsolete, and so does the service technician's training. When new equipment is installed, service technicians must demonstrate the intellectual agility to learn how to handle problems that might arise.

When asked what kind of people are best suited for this line of work, Arca replies, "task oriented, quantitatively smart, organized, and personable. Also, they need the ability to convey technical terms in writing and orally."

EMPLOYERS

Approximately 168,000 computer and office machine service technicians, including those who work on automated teller machines, are employed in the United States. Potential employers include computer companies and large corporations that need a staff devoted to repairing and maintaining their equipment; electronics, appliance, and office supply stores; electronic and precision equipment repair shops; computer systems design firms; government agencies, and Internet service providers. Many service technicians are employed by companies that contract their services to other businesses. Though work opportunities for service technicians are available nationwide, many jobs are located in large cities where computer companies and larger corporations are based.

STARTING OUT

If your school offers placement services, take advantage of them. Many times, school placements and counseling centers are privy to job openings that are filled before being advertised in the newspaper. Make sure your counselors know of any important preferences, such as location, specialization, and other requirements, so they can best match you to an employer. Do not forget to supply them with an updated resume.

There are also other avenues to take when searching for a job in this industry. Many jobs are advertised in the "Jobs" section of your local newspaper. Look under "Computers" or "Electronics." Also, inquire directly with the personnel department of companies that appeal to you and fill out an application. Trade association Web sites are good sources of job leads; many will post employment opportunities as well as allow you to post your resume.

ADVANCEMENT

Due to the growth of computer products and their influence over the business world, this industry offers a variety of advancement opportunities. Service technicians usually start by working on relatively simple maintenance and repair tasks. Over time, they start working on more complicated projects.

Experienced service technicians may advance to positions of increased responsibility, such as a crew supervisor or a departmental manager. Another advancement route is to become a sales representative for a computer manufacturing company. Technicians develop hands-on knowledge of particular machines and are thus often in the best position to advise potential buyers about important purchasing decisions. Some entrepreneurial-minded servicers might open their own repair business, which can be risky but can also provide many rewards. Unless they fill a certain market niche, technicians usually find it necessary to service a wide range of computers and office machines.

EARNINGS

The U.S. Department of Labor reports that the median hourly earnings for computer, automated teller, and office machine technicians were $17.54 in 2006. A technician earning this amount and working full time would have a yearly income of approximately $36,480. The department also reports that the lowest paid 10 percent of all computer and office machine service technicians (regardless of employer) earned less than $10.65 per hour ($22,150 annually). At the other end of the pay scale, 10 percent earned more than $27.36 per hour (approximately $56,910 annually). Those with certification are typically paid more than those without.

Standard work benefits for full-time technicians include health and life insurance and paid vacation and sick time, as well as a retirement plan. Most technicians are given travel stipends; some receive company cars.

WORK ENVIRONMENT

"I like the freedom of not working in a [typical] office environment and the short workweeks," says Joey Arca. Most service technicians, however, have unpredictable work schedules. Some weeks are quiet and may require fewer work hours. However, during a major computer problem, or worse yet, a breakdown, technicians are required to work around the clock to fix the problem as quickly as possible. Technicians spend a considerable amount of time on call, and must carry a pager in case of work emergencies.

Travel is an integral part of the job for many service technicians, many times amounting to 80 percent of the job time. Arca has even traveled to the Philippines, where he worked on the Tomahawk

Missile project at Clark Air Force Base. Since he is originally from the Philippines, he was able to combine work with a visit with friends and family.

OUTLOOK

According to the U.S. Department of Labor, employment for service technicians working with computer and office equipment should grow more slowly than the average for all occupations through 2014. Despite this prediction, demand for qualified and skilled technicians will be steady as corporations, the government, hospitals, and universities worldwide continue their reliance on computers to help manage their daily business. Opportunities are expected to be best for those with knowledge of electronics and working in computer repairs. Those working on office equipment, such as digital copiers, should find a demand for their services to repair and maintain increasingly technically sophisticated office machines.

FOR MORE INFORMATION

For information on internships, student membership, and the magazine Crossroads, *contact*

Association for Computing Machinery
1515 Broadway
New York, NY 10036-8901
Tel: 800-342-6626
Email: sigs@acm.org
http://www.acm.org

For information on certification, contact

Electronics Technicians Association International
5 Depot Street
Greencastle, IN 46135-8024
Tel: 800-288-3824
Email: eta@eta-i.org
http://www.eta-i.org

For industry and certification information, contact the following organizations:

ACES International
5241 Princess Anne Road, Suite 110
Virginia Beach, VA 23462-6310
Tel: 800-798-2237
http://www.acesinternational.org

CompTIA: The Computing Technology Industry Association
1815 South Meyers Road, Suite 300
Oakbrook Terrace, IL 60181-5228
Tel: 630-678-8300
http://www.comptia.org

Institute for Certification of Computing Professionals
2350 East Devon Avenue, Suite 115
Des Plaines, IL 60018-4610
Tel: 800-843-8227
Email: office@iccp.org
http://www.iccp.org

International Society of Certified Electronics Technicians
3608 Pershing Avenue
Fort Worth, TX 76107-4527
Tel: 800-946-0201
Email: info@iscet.org
http://www.iscet.org

Computer and Video Game Designers

QUICK FACTS

School Subjects
Art
Computer science

Personal Skills
Communication/ideas
Technical/scientific

Work Environment
Primarily indoors
Primarily one location

Minimum Education Level
Bachelor's degree

Salary Range
$43,486 to $69,813 to
$88,734

Certification or Licensing
None available

Outlook
About as fast as the average

DOT
N/A

GOE
01.04.02

NOC
2174

O*NET-SOC
27-1029.99

OVERVIEW

In the sector of the multibillion-dollar computer industry known as interactive entertainment and recreational computing, *computer and video game designers* create the ideas and interactivity for games. These games are played on various platforms, or media, such as video consoles and computers, and through online Internet subscriptions. They generate ideas for new game concepts, including sound effects, characters, story lines, and graphics.

Because the industry is fairly new, it is difficult to estimate how many people work as game designers. Around 90,000 people work within the video game industry as a whole. Designers either work for companies that make the games or create the games on their own and sell their ideas and programs to companies that produce them.

HISTORY

Computer and video game designers are a relatively new breed. The industry did not begin to develop until the 1960s and 1970s, when computer programmers at some large universities, big companies, and government labs began designing games on mainframe computers. Steve Russell was perhaps the first video game designer. In 1962, when he was in college, he made up a simple game called *Spacewar*. Graphics of space ships flew through a starry sky on the video screen, the object of the game being to shoot down enemy ships. Nolan Bushnell, another early designer, played *Spacewar* in college. In 1972 he put the first video game in an arcade; it was a game very much like *Spacewar*, and he called it *Computer Space*.

28

However, many users found the game difficult to play, so it was not a success.

Bruce Artwick published the first of many versions of *Flight Simulator*, and Bushnell later created *Pong*, a game that required the players to paddle electronic ping-pong balls back and forth across the video screen. *Pong* was a big hit, and players spent thousands of quarters in arcade machines all over the country playing it. Bushnell's company, Atari, had to hire more and more designers every week, including Steve Jobs, Alan Kay, and Chris Crawford. These early designers made games with text-based descriptions (that is, no graphics) of scenes and actions with interactivity done through a computer keyboard. Games called *Adventure*, *Star Trek*, and *Flight Simulator* were among the first that designers created. They used simple commands like "look at building" and "move west." Most games were designed for video machines; not until the late 1970s did specially equipped TVs and early personal computers (PCs) begin appearing.

In the late 1970s and early 1980s, designers working for Atari and Intellivision made games for home video systems, PCs, and video arcades. Many of these new games had graphics, sound, text, and animation. Designers of games like *Pac-Man*, *Donkey Kong*, and *Space Invaders* were successful and popular. They also started to make role-playing games like the famous *Dungeons and Dragons*. Richard Garriott created *Ultima*, another major role-playing game. Games began to feature the names and photos of their programmers on the packaging, giving credit to individual designers.

Workers at Electronic Arts began to focus on making games for PCs to take advantage of technology that included the computer keyboard, more memory, and floppy disks. They created games like *Carmen Sandiego* and *M.U.L.E.* In the mid- to late 1980s, new technology included more compact floppies, sound cards, and larger memory. Designers also had to create games that would work on more than just one platform—PCs, Apple computers, and 64-bit video game machines.

In the 1990s, Electronic Arts started to hire teams of designers instead of "lone wolf" individuals (those who design games from start to finish independently). Larger teams were needed because games became more complex; design teams would include not only programmers but also artists, musicians, writers, and animators. Designers made such breakthroughs as using more entertaining graphics, creating more depth in role-playing games, using virtual reality in sports games, and using more visual realism in racing games and flight simulators. This new breed of designers created games using techniques like Assembly, C, and HyperCard. By 1994, designers began to use CD-ROM technology to its fullest. In only a few months, *Doom* was a hit. Designers of this game gave players the chance to alter it themselves at various levels, including choices of weapons and enemies. *Doom* still has fans worldwide.

The success of shareware (software that is given away to attract users to want to buy more complete software) has influenced the return of smaller groups of designers. Even the lone wolf is coming back, using shareware and better authoring tools such as sound libraries and complex multimedia development environments. Some designers are finding that they work best on their own or in small teams.

What is on the horizon for game designers? More multiplayer games; virtual reality; improved technology in coprocessors, chips, hardware, and sound fonts; and "persistent worlds," where online games are influenced by and evolve from players' actions. These new types of games require that designers know more and more complex code so that games can "react" to their multiple players.

THE JOB

Designing games involves programming code as well as creating stories, graphics, and sound effects. It is a very creative process, requiring imagination and computer and communication skills to develop games that are interactive and entertaining. As mentioned earlier, some game designers work on their own and try to sell their designs to companies that produce and distribute games; others are employees of companies such as Electronic Arts, Broderbund, and many others. Whether designers work alone or for a company, their aim is to create games that get players involved. Game players want to have fun, be challenged, and sometimes learn something along the way.

Each game must have a story line as well as graphics and sound that will entertain and engage the players. Story lines are situations that the players will find themselves in and make decisions about. Designers develop a plan for combining the story or concept, music or other sound effects, and graphics. They design rules to make it fun, challenging, or educational, and they create characters for the stories or circumstances, worlds in which these characters live, and problems or situations these characters will face.

One of the first steps is to identify the audience that will be playing the game. How old are the players? What kinds of things are they interested in? What kind of game will it be: action, adventure, "edutainment," role-playing, or sports? And which platform will the game use: video game system (e.g., Nintendo), computer (e.g., Macintosh), or online (Internet via subscription)?

The next steps are to create a design proposal, a preliminary design, and a final game design. The proposal is a brief summary of what the game involves. The preliminary design goes much further, outlining in more detail what the concept is (the story of the game); how the players get involved; what sound effects, graphics, and other elements will be included (What will the screen look like? What kinds of sound effects should the player hear?); and what productivity tools (such as word processors, database programs, spreadsheet programs, flow-charting programs, and prototyping programs) the designer intends to use to create these elements. Independent designers submit a product idea and design proposal to a publisher along with a cover letter and resume. Employees work as part of a team to create the proposal and design. Teamwork might include brainstorming sessions to come up with ideas, as well as involvement in market research (surveying the players who will be interested in the game).

The final game design details the basic idea, the plot, and every section of the game, including the startup process, all the scenes (such as innings for baseball games and maps for edutainment games), and all the universal elements (such as rules for scoring, names of characters, and a sound effect that occurs every time something specific happens). The story, characters, worlds, and maps are documented. The game design also includes details of the logic of the game, its algorithms (the step-by-step procedures for solving the problems the players will encounter), and its rules; the methods the player will use to load the game, start it up, score, win, lose, save, stop, and play again; the graphic design, including storyboards and sample art; and the audio design. The designer might also include marketing ideas and proposed follow-up games.

Designers interact with other workers and technologists involved in the game design project, including programmers, audio engineers, artists, and even *asset managers,* who coordinate the collecting, engineering, and distribution of physical assets to the *production team* (the people who will actually produce the physical CD-ROM or DVD).

Designers need to understand games and their various forms, think up new ideas, and experiment with and evaluate new designs. They assemble the separate elements (text, art, sound, and video) of a game into a complete, interactive form, following through with careful planning and preparation (such as sketching out scripts, storyboards, and design documents). They write an implementation plan and guidelines. (How will designers manage the process? How much will it cost to design the game? How long will the guidelines be—five pages? 300?) Finally, they amend designs at every stage, solving problems and answering questions.

Computer and video game designers often keep scrapbooks, notes, and journals of interesting ideas and other bits of information. They collect potential game material and even catalog ideas, videos, movies, pictures, stories, character descriptions, music clips, sound effects, animation sequences, and interface techniques. The average time it takes to design a game, including all the elements and stages just described, can be from about six to 18 months.

REQUIREMENTS

High School

If you like to play video or computer games, you are already familiar with them. You will also need to learn a programming language like C++ or Java, and you'll need a good working knowledge of the hardware platform for which you plan to develop your games (video, computer, online). In high school, learn as much as you can about computers: how they work, what kinds there are, how to program them, and any languages you can learn. You should also take physics, chemistry, and computer science. Since designers are creative, take courses such as art, literature, and music as well.

Postsecondary Training

Although strictly speaking you don't have to have a college degree to be a game designer, most companies are looking for creative people who also have a degree. Having one represents that you've been actively involved in intense, creative work; that you can work with others and follow through on assignments; and, of course, that

Industry Stats

- Computer and video game software sales totaled $7.4 billion in 2006—a 6 percent increase from 2005.
- The computer and video game industry has released more than 7,000 titles since 1994.
- Sixty-two percent of game players are male.
- The average game player is 33 years old.
- Eighty percent of parents who play computer and video games report that they play games with their children.
- Forty-nine percent of gamers play online games one or more hours per week.
- The industry has a bright future, at least according to current game players. Fifty-three percent of game players today say they will be playing as much or more in 10 years.

Source: Entertainment Software Association

you've learned what there is to know about programming, computer architecture (including input devices, processing devices, memory and storage devices, and output devices), and software engineering. Employers want to know that you've had some practical experience in design.

A growing number of schools offer courses or degrees in game design. The University of North Texas, for example, has a Laboratory for Recreational Computing (LARC) that offers two senior elective courses, Game Programming and Advanced Game Programming. For more information, visit http://larc.csci.unt.edu. One of the best-known degree-granting schools is DigiPen Institute of Technology (http://www.digipen.edu) in Redmond, Wash., with programs both at the associate, bachelor's, and master's level. Another example is the Entertainment Technology Center (ETC) at Carnegie Mellon University. Video game designer Shawn Patton holds a master's degree in entertainment technology from the ETC. He describes the ETC as "a mixture of technologists and artists." Much of the ETC's courses involve collaborative efforts, with both students and professor providing feedback on group projects. Patton says, "The ETC grants its students the ability to experience real work with the safety net of being able to fail (and not lose your job) as long as you learn from that failure." (Visit http://www.etc.cmu.edu for more information on the ETC.) For a list of schools in the United States, visit http://www.igda.org/breakingin/resource_schools.php.

The college courses you should take include programming (including assembly level), computer architecture, software engineering, computer graphics, data structures, algorithms, communication networks, artificial intelligence (AI) and expert systems, interface systems, mathematics, and physics.

According to Professor Ian Parberry of the LARC, the quality of your education depends a lot on you. "You must take control of your education, seek out the best professors, and go beyond the material presented in class. What you have a right to expect from an undergraduate computer science degree is a grasp of the fundamental concepts of computer science and enough practical skills to be able to grow, learn, and thrive in any computational environment, be it computer games or otherwise."

Other Requirements

One major requirement for game design is that you must love to play computer games. You need to keep up with technology, which changes fast. Although you might not always use them, you need to have a variety of skills, such as writing stories, programming, and designing sound effects.

You must also have vision and the ability to identify your players and anticipate their every move in your game. You'll also have to be able to communicate well with programmers, writers, artists, musicians, electronics engineers, production workers, and others.

You must have the endurance to see a project through from beginning to end and also be able to recognize when a design should be scrapped.

Shawn Patton also advises, "An analytical mind is a must. If you like solving problems by thinking about all the variables, all the possible outcomes of your actions, and then applying those actions in a clear and concise manner, you probably have an analytical mind."

EXPLORING

One of the best ways to learn about game design is to try to develop copies of easy games, such as *Pong* and *Pac-Man*, or try to change a game that has an editor. (Games like *Klik & Play, Empire,* and *Doom* allow players to modify them to create new circumstances and settings.)

For high school students interested in finding out more about how video games and animations are produced, the DigiPen Institute of Technology offers a summer workshop. Two-week courses are offered during July and August, providing hands-on experience and advice on courses to take in high school to prepare yourself for postsecondary training.

Writing your own stories, puzzles, and games helps develop storytelling and problem-solving skills. Magazines such as *Computer Graphics World* (http://www.cgw.com) and *Game Developer* (http://www.gdmag.com) have articles about digital video and high-end imaging and other technical and design information.

Shawn Patton recommends "tinkering in your free time: If you have a great idea for a game or an application, sit down and try to program it in whatever language you know/have at your disposal. Learning by doing is great in computer science."

EMPLOYERS

Software publishers (such as Electronic Arts and Activision) are found throughout the country, though most are located in California, New York, Washington, and Illinois. Electronic Arts is the largest independent publisher of interactive entertainment, including several development studios; the company is known worldwide. Big media companies such as Disney have also opened interactive entertainment departments. Jobs should be available at these companies as well as with online services and interactive networks, which are growing rapidly.

Some companies are involved in producing games only for video; others produce only for computers; others make games for various platforms.

STARTING OUT

There are a couple of ways to begin earning money as a game designer: independently or as an employee of a company. It is more realistic to get any creative job you can in the industry (for example, as an artist, a play tester, a programmer, or a writer) and learn as you go, developing your design skills as you work your way up to the level of designer.

Contact company Web sites and sites that advertise job openings, such as Game Jobs (http://www.gamejobs.com).

In addition to a professional resume, it is a good idea to have your own Web site, where you can showcase your demos. Make sure you have designed at least one demo or have an impressive portfolio of design ideas and documents.

Other ways to find a job in the industry include going to job fairs (such as the Game Developers Conference, http://www.gdconf.com), where you find recruiters looking for creative people to work at their companies, and checking in with online user groups, which often post jobs on the Internet.

Also consider looking for an internship to prepare for this career. Many software and entertainment companies hire interns for short-term assignments. For example, Shawn Patton completed an internship at Walt Disney Imagineering 9WDI in Glendale, Calif., where he helped develop the game *Toontown Online* (http://www.toon town.com). Regarding his internship, Patton says, "What I enjoyed the most about WDI was that I was able to work on code that was immediately released to the public, who then gave feedback on it. . . . I liked knowing that something I made was being used by and entertaining someone else. That's a feeling I hope to find in whatever job I end up having."

ADVANCEMENT

Just as with many jobs, to have better opportunities to advance their position and possibly earn more money, computer and video game designers have to keep up with technology. They must be willing to learn more about design, the industry, and even financial and legal matters involved in development.

Becoming and remaining great at their job may be a career-long endeavor for computer and video game designers, or just a stepping-stone to another area of interactive entertainment. Some designers start out as artists, writers, or programmers, learning enough in these jobs to eventually design. For example, a person entering this career may begin as a 3-D animation modeler and work on enough game life cycles to understand what it takes to be a game designer. He or she may decide to specialize in another area, such as sound effects or even budgeting.

Some designers rise to management positions, such as president or vice president of a software publisher. Others write for magazines and books, teach, or establish their own game companies.

EARNINGS

Most development companies spend up to two years designing a game even before any of the mechanics (such as writing final code and drawing final graphics) begin; more complex games take even longer. Companies budget $1–3 million for developing just one game. If the game is a success, designers are often rewarded with bonuses. In addition to bonuses or royalties (the percentage of profits designers receive from each game that is sold), designers' salaries are affected by their amount of professional experience, their location in the country, and the size of their employer. Gama Network, an organization serving electronic games developers, surveyed subscribers, members, and attendees of its three divisions (*Game Developer* magazine, Gamasutra.com, and the Game Developers Conference) to find out what professionals in the game development industry were earning. The survey reveals that in 2005 game designers with less than three years of experience had an average annual salary of approximately $43,486. Those with three to six years of experience averaged $54,777 annually, and those with more than six years of experience averaged $69,813 per year. Lead designers/creative directors earned higher salaries, ranging from $72,125 for those with three to six years of experience to $88,734 for workers with six or more years of experience in the field. It is important to note that these salaries are averages, and some designers (especially those at the beginning stages of their careers) earn less than these amounts. These figures, however, provide a useful guide for the range of earnings available.

Any major software publisher will likely provide benefits such as medical insurance, paid vacations, and retirement plans. Designers who are self-employed must provide their own benefits.

WORK ENVIRONMENT

Computer and video game designers work in office settings, whether at a large company or a home studio. At some companies, artists and designers sometimes find themselves working 24 or 48 hours at a time, so the office areas are set up with sleeping couches and other areas where employees can relax. Because the game development industry is competitive, many designers find themselves under a lot of pressure from deadlines, design problems, and budget concerns.

OUTLOOK

Computer and video games are a fast-growing segment of the U.S. entertainment industry. In fact, the Entertainment Software Association reports that sales of computer and video game software reached $7.6 billion in 2006. As the demand for new games, more sophisticated games, and games to be played on new systems grows, more and more companies will hire skilled people to create and perfect these products. Opportunities for game designers, therefore, should be good.

In any case, game development is popular; the Entertainment Software Association estimates that about 60 percent of American heads of households play computer and video games. People in the industry expect more and more integration of interactive entertainment into mainstream society. Online development tools such as engines, graphic and sound libraries, and programming languages such as Java will probably create opportunities for new types of products that can feature game components.

FOR MORE INFORMATION

For information on associate and bachelor of science degrees in computer animation and simulation, contact

DigiPen Institute of Technology
5001-150th Avenue, NE
Redmond, WA 98052-5170
Tel: 866-478-5236
Email: info@digipen.edu
http://www.digipen.edu

For industry information, contact

Entertainment Software Association
575 7th Street, NW, Suite 300
Washington, DC 20004-1611

Email: esa@theesa.com
http://www.theesa.com

For comprehensive career information, including Breaking In: Preparing For Your Career in Games, *visit IGDA's Web site:*
International Game Developers Association (IGDA)
19 Mantua Road
Mt. Royal, NJ 08061-1006
Tel: 856-423-2990
Email: contact@igda.org
http://www.igda.org

Computer Network Administrators

OVERVIEW

Computer network administrators, or network specialists, design, install, and support an organization's local area network (LAN), wide area network (WAN), network segment, or Internet or Intranet system. They maintain network hardware and software, analyze problems, and monitor the network to ensure availability to system users. Administrators also might plan, coordinate, and implement network security measures, including firewalls. Approximately 278,000 computer network and systems administrators work in the United States.

HISTORY

The first substantial developments in modern computer technology took place in the mid-twentieth century. After World War II, it was thought that the use of computers would be limited to large government projects, such as the U.S. Census, because computers at this time were enormous (they easily took up the space of entire warehouses).

Smaller and less expensive computers were made possible due to the introduction of semiconductors. Businesses began using computers in their operations as early as 1954. Within 30 years, computers revolutionized the way people worked, played, and shopped. Today, computers are everywhere, from businesses of all kinds to government agencies, charitable organizations, and private homes. Over the years, technology has continued to shrink the size of computers and increase computer speed at an unprecedented rate.

QUICK FACTS

School Subjects
Computer science
Mathematics

Personal Skills
Helping/teaching
Leadership/management
Technical/scientific

Work Environment
Primarily indoors
Primarily one location

Minimum Education Level
Bachelor's degree

Salary Range
$38,610 to $62,130 to $97,080+

Certification or Licensing
Recommended

Outlook
Much faster than the average

DOT
031

GOE
02.06.01

NOC
0213

O*NET-SOC
15-1071.00, 15-1081.00

The first commercially used computers were composed of a system of several big mainframe computers. These computers were located in special rooms and several independent terminals around the office. Though efficient and effective, the mainframe had several problems. One problem was the update delay, or the time lapse, between when an employee input information into a computer and when that information became available to other employees. Although advances in hardware technology have begun addressing this and other problems of mainframes, many computer companies and businesses have now turned to networking instead.

Rather than relying on a mainframe system, computer networks use a network server to centralize the processing capacity of several different computers and other related equipment (known as peripherals). In a network, terminals and other computers are linked directly to the server. This direct link provides other computer users with instantaneous access to the information. The increased need for qualified computer network administrators to oversee network operations has paralleled the growth of computer networking.

The use of networks has grown rapidly as more companies move from mainframe computers to client-server networks or from paper-based systems to automated record-keeping using networked databases. The rapid growth of Internet technology has created a new area that also is in need of networking professionals.

THE JOB

Businesses use computer networks for several reasons. One important reason is that networks make it easy for many employees to share hardware and software as well as printers, fax machines, and modems. For example, it would be very expensive to buy individual copies of word-processing programs for each employee in a company. By investing in a network version of the software that all employees can access, companies can often save a lot of money. Also, businesses that rely on databases for daily operations use networks to allow authorized personnel quick and easy access to the most updated version of the database.

Networks vary greatly in size; even just two computers connected together are considered a network. They can also be extremely large and complex, involving hundreds of computer terminals in various geographical locations around the world. A good example of a large network is the Internet, which is a system that allows people from every corner of the globe to access millions of pieces of information about any subject under the sun. Besides varying in size, networks are all at least slightly different in terms of configuration, or what the network is designed to do; businesses customize networks to meet their specific needs. All networks, regardless of size or configuration, experience problems. For example, communications with certain equipment can break down, users might need extra training or forget their passwords, backup files may be lost, or new software might need to be installed and configured. Whatever the crisis, computer network administrators must know the network system well enough to diagnose and fix the problem.

Computer network administrators or specialists may hold one or several networking responsibilities. The specific job duties assigned to one person depend on the nature and scope of the employer. For example, in a medium-size company that uses computers only minimally, a computer network specialist might be expected to do everything associated with the office computer system. In larger companies with more sophisticated computing systems, computer network administrators are likely to hold narrower and better-defined responsibilities. The following descriptions highlight the different kinds of computer network administrators.

In the narrowest sense, computer network administrators are responsible for adding and deleting files to the network server, a centralized computer. Among other things, the server stores the software applications used by network users on a daily basis. Administrators update files from the database, electronic mail, and word-processing applications. They are also responsible for making sure that printing jobs run properly. This task entails telling the server where the printer is and establishing a printing queue, or line, designating which print jobs have priority.

Another duty of some network administrators is setting up user access. Since businesses store confidential information on the server, users typically have access to only a limited number of applications. Network administrators tell the computer who can use which programs and when they can use them. They create a series of passwords to secure the system against internal and external spying. They also troubleshoot problems and questions encountered by staff members.

In companies with large computer systems, *network security specialists* concentrate solely on system security. They set up and monitor user access and update security files as needed. For example, it is very important in universities that only certain administrative personnel have the ability to change student grades on the database. Network security specialists must protect the system from unauthorized grade changes. Network security specialists grant new passwords to users who forget them, record all nonauthorized entries, report unauthorized users to appropriate management, and change any files that have been tampered with. They also maintain security files with information about each employee.

Network control operators are in charge of all network communications, most of which operate over telephone lines or fiber optic cables. When users encounter communications problems, they call the network control operator. A typical communications problem occurs when a user cannot send or receive files from other computers. Since users seldom have a high level of technical expertise on the network, the network control operator knows how to ask appropriate questions in user-friendly language to determine the source of the problem. If it is not a user error, the network control operator checks the accuracy of computer files, verifies that modems are functioning properly, and runs noise tests on the communications lines using special equipment. As with all network specialists, if the problem proves to be too difficult for the network control operator to resolve, he or she seeks help directly from the manufacturer or warranty company.

Network control operators also keep detailed records of the number of communications transactions made, the number and nature of network errors, and the methods used to resolve them. These records help them address problems as they arise in the future.

Network systems administrators that specialize in Internet technology are essential to its success. One of their responsibilities is to prepare servers for use and link them together so others can place things on them. Under the supervision of the *Webmaster,* the systems administrator might set aside areas on a server for particular types of information, such as documents, graphics, or audio. At sites that are set up to handle secure credit card transactions, administrators are responsible for setting up the secure server that handles this job. They also monitor site traffic and take the necessary steps to ensure uninterrupted operation. In some cases, the solution is to provide additional space on the server. In others, the only solution might be to increase bandwidth by upgrading the telephone line linking the site to the Internet.

REQUIREMENTS

High School

In high school, take as many courses as possible in computer science, mathematics, and science, which provide a solid foundation in computer basics and analytical-thinking skills. You should also practice your verbal and written communications skills in English and speech classes. Business courses are valuable in that they can give you an understanding of how important business decisions, especially those concerning investment in computer equipment, are made.

Postsecondary Training

Most network jobs require at least a bachelor's degree in computer science or computer engineering. More specialized positions require an advanced degree. Workers with a college education are more likely to deal with the theoretical aspects of computer networking and are more likely to be promoted to management positions. Opportunities in computer design, systems analysis, and computer programming, for example, are open only to college graduates. If you are interested in this field, you should also pursue postsecondary training in network administration or network engineering.

"I believe that you cannot have enough education and that it should be an ongoing thing," says Nancy Nelson, a network administrator at Baxter Healthcare Corporation in Deerfield, Ill. "You can learn a lot on your own, but I think you miss out on a lot if you don't get the formal education. Most companies don't even look at a resume that doesn't have a degree. Keeping up with technology can be very rewarding."

Certification or Licensing

Besides the technical/vocational schools that offer courses related to computer networking, several major companies offer professionally taught courses and nationally recognized certification; chief among them are Novell and Microsoft. The certified network professional program supports and complements the aforementioned vendor product certifications. Offered by the Network Professional Association, the program covers fundamental knowledge in client operating systems, microcomputer hardware platforms, network operating system fundamentals, protocols, and topologies.

Commercial postsecondary training programs are flexible. You can complete courses at your own pace, but you must take all parts of the certification test within one year. You may attend classes at any one of many educational sites around the country or you can study on your own. Many students find certification exams difficult.

Other Requirements

Continuing education for any computer profession is crucial to success. Many companies will require you to keep up to date on new technological advances by attending classes, workshops, and seminars throughout the year. Also, many companies and professional associations update network specialists through newsletters, other periodicals, and online bulletin boards.

Computer work is complex, detailed, and often very frustrating. In order to succeed in this field, you must be well organized and patient. You should enjoy challenges and problem solving, and you should be a logical thinker. You must also be able to communicate complex ideas in simple terms, as well as be able to work well under pressure and deadlines. As a network specialist, you should be naturally curious about the computing field; you must always be willing to learn more about new and different technologies.

EXPLORING

"One of the greatest learning experiences in this field is just unpacking a new computer, setting it up, and getting connected to the Internet, continually asking yourself how and why as you go," says Dan Creedon, a network administrator at Nesbitt Burns Securities in Chicago.

If you are interested in computer networking you should join computer clubs at school and community centers and surf the Internet or other online services. Ask your school administration about the possibility of working with the school system's network specialists for a day or longer. Parents' or friends' employers might also be a good place to find this type of opportunity.

If seeking part-time jobs, apply for those that include computer work. Though you will not find networking positions, any experience on computers will increase your general computing knowledge. In addition, once employed, you can actively seek exposure to the other computer functions in the business.

You might also try volunteering at local-area charities that use computer networks in their office. Because many charities have small budgets, they may offer more opportunities to gain experience with some of the simpler networking tasks. In addition, experiment by creating networks with your own computer, those of your friends, and any printers, modems, and faxes that you have access to.

You should play around on computers as much as possible. Read and learn from any resource you can, such as magazines, newsletters, and online bulletin boards.

EMPLOYERS

Approximately 278,000 computer network and systems administrators are employed in the United States. Any company or organization that uses computer networks in its business employs network administrators. These include insurance companies, banks, financial institutions, health care organizations, federal and state governments, universities, and other corporations that rely on networking. Also, since smaller companies are moving to client-server models, more opportunities at almost any kind of business are becoming available.

STARTING OUT

There are several ways to obtain a position as a computer network specialist. If you are a student in a technical school or university, take advantage of your campus career services office. Check regularly for internship postings, job listings, and notices of on-campus recruitment. Career services offices are also valuable resources for resume tips and interviewing techniques. Internships and summer jobs with corporations are always beneficial and provide experience that will give you the edge over your competition. General computer job fairs are also held throughout the year in larger cities.

There are many online career sites listed on the World Wide Web that post job openings, salary surveys, and current employment trends. The Web also has online publications that deal specifically with computer jobs. You can also obtain information from computer organizations, such as the IEEE Computer Society and the Network Professional Association (see contact information at the end of this article).

When a job opportunity arises, you should send a cover letter and resume to the company promptly. Follow up your mailing with a phone call about one week later. If interested, the company recruiter will call you to ask questions and possibly arrange an interview. The commercial sponsors of network certification, such as Novell and Microsoft, also publish newsletters that list current job openings in the field. The same information is distributed through online bulletin boards and on the Internet as well. Otherwise, you can scan the classified ads in local newspapers and computer magazines or work with an employment agency to find such a position.

Individuals already employed but wishing to move into computer networking should investigate the possibility of tuition reimbursement from their employer for network certification. Many large companies have this type of program, which allows employees to train in a field that would benefit company operations. After successfully completing classes or certification, individuals are better qualified for related job openings in their own company and more likely to be hired into them.

ADVANCEMENT

"I would say that as much as a person is willing to learn is really the amount of advancement opportunities that are open to them," notes Dan Creedon. Among the professional options available are promotion to network manager or movement into network engineering. *Network engineers* design, test, and evaluate network systems, such as LAN, WAN, Internet, and other data communications systems.

They also perform modeling, analysis, and planning. Network engineers might also research related products and make hardware and software recommendations.

Network specialists also have the option of going into a different area of computing. They can become computer programmers, systems analysts, software engineers, or multimedia professionals. All of these promotions require additional education and solid computer experience.

EARNINGS

Factors such as the size and type of employer, the administrator's experience, and specific job duties influence the earnings of network administrators. According to the U.S. Department of Labor, the median yearly income for computer network and systems administrators was $62,130 in 2006. The lowest paid 10 percent made less than $38,610 per year, and the highest paid 10 percent earned more than $97,080 annually that same year.

Most computer network administrators are employed by companies that offer the full range of benefits, including health insurance, paid vacation, and sick leave. In addition, many companies have tuition reimbursement programs for employees seeking to pursue education or professional certification.

WORK ENVIRONMENT

Computer network administrators work indoors in a comfortable office environment. Their work is generally fast paced and can be frustrating at times. Some tasks, however, are routine and might get a little boring after a while. But many times, network specialists are required to work under a lot of pressure. If the network goes down, for example, the company is losing money, and it is the network specialist's job to get it up and running as fast as possible. The specialist must be able to remember complicated relationships and many details accurately and quickly. Specialists are also called on to deal effectively with the many complaints from network users.

When working on the installation of a new system, many network specialists are required to work overtime until it is fully operational. This usually includes long and frequent meetings. During initial operations of the system, some network specialists may be on call during other shifts for when problems arise, or they may have to train network users during off hours.

One other potential source of frustration is communications with other employees. Network specialists deal every day with people who usually don't understand the system as well as they do. Network administrators must be able to communicate at different levels of understanding.

OUTLOOK

The U.S. Department of Labor projects that employment for computer network and systems administrators will grow much faster than the average for all occupations through 2014. Network administrators are in high demand, particularly those with Internet experience. "Technology is constantly changing," Nancy Nelson says. "It is hard to tell where it will lead in the future. I think that the Internet and all of its pieces will be the place to focus on." As more and more companies and organizations discover the economic and convenience advantages linked to using computer networks at all levels of operations, the demand for well-trained network specialists will increase. Job opportunities should be best for those with certification and up-to-date training.

FOR MORE INFORMATION

For information on internships, student membership, and the student magazine Crossroads, *contact*
Association for Computing Machinery
1515 Broadway
New York, NY 10036-8901
Tel: 800-342-6626
Email: sigs@acm.org
http://www.acm.org

For information on career opportunities for women in computing, contact
Association for Women in Computing
41 Sutter Street, Suite 1006
San Francisco, CA 94104-5414
Tel: 415-905-4663
Email: info@awc-hq.org
http://www.awc-hq.org

For information on scholarships, student membership, and to read Careers in Computer Science and Computer Engineering, *visit the IEEE's Web site:*
IEEE Computer Society
1730 Massachusetts Avenue, NW

Washington, DC 20036-1992
Tel: 202-371-0101
Email: membership@computer.org
http://www.computer.org

For information on certification, contact
Network Professional Association
1401 Hermes Lane
San Diego, CA 92154-2721
Tel: 888-NPA-NPA0
http://www.npanet.org

For information on systems administration, contact
SAGE
c/o USENIX, the Advanced Computing Systems Association
2560 9th Street, Suite 215
Berkeley, CA 94710-2565
Tel: 510-528-8649
Email: office@usenix.org
http://www.sage.org

—————— INTERVIEW ——————

Guy Hembroff is an assistant professor and chair of the Computer Network System Administration (CNSA) program at Michigan Technological University (http://www.tech.mtu.edu/cnsa) in Houghton, Michigan. He discussed the field with the editors of Careers in Focus: Computers.

Q. Please tell us about your program and your background in the field.

A. The Computer Network System Administration program prepares students for positions such as network/systems engineers, network integration engineers, network security analysts, network/systems administrators, e-commerce developers, database administrators, and voice over IP (VoIP) engineers. We offer a variety of internships/co-ops that stem from network engineering, system administration, and network security. Organizations such as Harley-Davidson, Los Alamos National Security Lab, and Toyota have hired our students for internships/co-ops.

I have worked within industry as a systems engineer and advanced network engineer. Although I still consult in the field, my research areas are securing mobile devices and advanced network engineering architectures.

Q. What is one thing that young people may not know about a career in computer networking and system administration?

A. Students may not know the extent of how integrated our program is associated with network and computer security. This is a very popular area that continues to grow. Our students are educated with advanced conceptual security knowledge (through lectures) and "hands-on" security experience (through intensive and advanced labs).

Q. What types of students pursue study in your program?

A. Students who are very interested in computers and networking technology. In addition, due to the field of study and the lab intensity of our program, students who excel in our program are those who have good problem solving skills, the ability to think outside-the-box, and are able to transition theory into "real-world" applications and solutions.

Q. What advice would you give to graduates of your program?

A. Try to attain as much "real-world" experience as possible through internships and co-ops. This also gives the students a very good idea of what to expect within industry, along with great experience that will make them more marketable.

Q. What is the employment outlook for the field? What areas of the field will be especially promising in the future?

A. The employment outlook is very good. Areas such as network security, network engineering, and VoIP are fields that are growing rapidly.

Computer Programmers

QUICK FACTS

School Subjects
Computer science
Mathematics

Personal Skills
Communication/ideas
Technical/scientific

Work Environment
Primarily indoors
Primarily one location

Minimum Education Level
Associate's degree

Salary Range
$38,460 to $65,510 to
$106,610+

Certification or Licensing
Voluntary

Outlook
More slowly than the average

DOT
030

GOE
02.06.01

NOC
2174

O*NET-SOC
15-1021.00

OVERVIEW

Computer programmers work in the field of electronic data processing. They write instructions that tell computers what to do in a computer language, or code, that the computer understands. Maintenance tasks include giving computers instructions on how to allocate time to various jobs they receive from computer terminals and making sure that these assignments are performed properly. There are approximately 455,000 computer programmers employed in the United States, and 25,000 of these programmers are self-employed.

HISTORY

Data processing systems and their support personnel are a product of World War II. The amount of information that had to be compiled and organized for war efforts became so great that it was not possible for people to collect it and put it in order in time for the necessary decisions to be made. It was obvious that a quicker way had to be devised to gather and organize information if decisions based on logic and not on guesses were to be made.

After the war, the new computer technology was put to use in other government operations as well as in businesses. The first computer used in a civilian capacity was installed by the Bureau of the Census in 1951 in order to help compile data from the 1950 census. At this time, computers were so large, cumbersome, and energy draining that the only practical use for them was thought to be large projects such as the census. However, three years later the first computer was installed by a business firm. Since 1954, many thousands of data processing systems have been installed in government agencies, industrial firms, banks, insurance agencies, educational systems, publishing houses, colleges and universities, and scientific laboratories.

Although computers seem capable of doing just about anything, one thing is still as true of computers today as it was of the first computer 60 years ago—they cannot think for themselves! Computers are machines that can only do exactly what they are told. This requires a small army of qualified computer programmers who understand computer languages well enough to give computers instructions on what to do, when, and how in order to meet the needs of government, business, and individuals. Some programmers are currently working on artificial intelligence, or computers that can in fact "think" for themselves and make humanlike decisions, but perfection of such technology is far off. As long as there are computers and new computer applications, there will be a constant need for programmers.

THE JOB

Broadly speaking, there are two types of computer programmers. *Systems programmers* maintain the instructions, called programs or software, that control the entire computer system, including both the central processing unit and the equipment with which it communicates, such as terminals, printers, and disk drives. *Applications programmers* write the software to handle specific jobs and may specialize in engineering, scientific, or business programs. Some of the latter specialists may be designated *chief business programmers*, who supervise the work of other business programmers.

Programmers are often given program specifications prepared by systems analysts, who list in detail the steps the computer must follow in order to complete a given task. Programmers then code these instructions in a computer language the computer understands. In smaller companies, analysis and programming may be handled by the same person, called a *programmer-analyst.*

Before actually writing the computer program, a programmer must analyze the work request, understand the current problem and desired resolution, decide on an approach to the problem, and plan what the machine will have to do to produce the required results. Programmers prepare a flowchart to show the steps in sequence that the machine must make. They must pay attention to minute details and instruct the machine in each step of the process.

These instructions are then coded in one of several programming languages, such as BASIC, COBOL, FORTRAN, PASCAL, RPG, CSP, C++, and Java. When the program is completed, the programmer tests its working practicality by running it on simulated data. If the machine responds according to expectations, actual data will be fed into it and the program will be activated. If the computer does not respond as anticipated, the program will have to be debugged, that is, examined for errors that must be eliminated. Finally, the programmer prepares an instruction sheet for the computer operator who will run the program.

The programmer's job concerns both an overall picture of the problem at hand and the minute detail of potential solutions. Programmers work from two points of view: from that of the people who need certain results and from that of technological problem solving. The work is divided equally between meeting the needs of other people and comprehending the capabilities of the machines.

Electronic data systems involve more than just one machine. Depending on the kind of system being used, the operation may require other machines such as printers or other peripherals. Introducing a new piece of equipment to an existing system often requires programmers to rewrite many programs.

Programmers may specialize in certain types of work, depending on the kind of problem to be solved and on the employer. Making a program for a payroll is, for example, very different from programming the study of structures of chemical compounds. Programmers who specialize in a certain field or industry generally have education or experience in that area before they are promoted to senior programming positions. *Information system programmers* specialize in programs for storing and retrieving physical science, engineering, or medical information; text analysis; and language, law, military, or library science data. As the information superhighway continues to grow, information system programmers have increased opportunities in online businesses, such as those of LexisNexis, Westlaw, America Online, Microsoft, and many others.

Process control programmers develop programs for systems that control automatic operations for commercial and industrial enterprises, such as steelmaking, sanitation plants, combustion systems, computerized production testing, or automatic truck loading. *Numerical control tool programmers* program the tape that controls the machining of automatic machine tools.

REQUIREMENTS

High School

In high school you should take any computer programming or computer science courses available. You should also concentrate on math, science, and schematic drawing courses, since these subjects directly prepare students for careers in computer programming.

Postsecondary Training

Most employers prefer their programmers to be college graduates. In the past, as the field was first taking shape, employers were known to hire people with some formal education and little or no experience but determination and the ability to learn quickly. As the market becomes saturated with individuals wishing to break into this field, however, a college degree is becoming increasingly important. The U.S. Department of Labor reports that more than 68 precent of computer programmers held a bachelor's degree in 2006.

Many personnel officers administer aptitude tests to determine potential for programming work. Some employers send new employees to computer schools or in-house training sessions before the employees are considered qualified to assume programming responsibilities. Training periods may last as long as a few weeks, months, or even a year.

Many junior and community colleges also offer two-year associate's degree programs in data processing, computer programming, and other computer-related technologies.

Most four-year colleges and universities have computer science departments with a variety of computer-related majors, any of which could prepare a student for a career in programming. Employers who require a college degree often do not express a preference as to major field of study, although mathematics or computer science is highly favored. Other acceptable majors may be business administration, accounting, engineering, or physics. Entrance requirements for jobs with the government are much the same as those in private industry.

Certification or Licensing

Students who choose to obtain a two-year degree might consider becoming certified by the Institute for Certification of Computing Professionals, whose address is listed at the end of this article. Although it is not required, certification may boost an individual's attractiveness to employers during the job search.

Other Requirements

Personal qualifications such as a high degree of reasoning ability, patience, and persistence, as well as an aptitude for mathematics, are important for computer programmers. Some employers whose work is highly technical require that programmers be qualified in the area in which the firm or agency operates. Engineering firms, for example, prefer young people with an engineering background and are willing to train them in some programming techniques. For other firms, such as banks, consumer-level knowledge of the services that banks offer may be sufficient background for incoming programmers.

EXPLORING

If you are interested in becoming a computer programmer, you might visit a large bank or insurance company in your community and seek an appointment to talk with one of the programmers on the staff. You may be able to visit the data processing center and see the machines in operation. You might also talk with a sales representative from one of the large manufacturers of data processing equipment and request whatever brochures or pamphlets the company publishes.

It is a good idea to start early and get some hands-on experience operating and programming a computer. A trip to the local library or bookstore is likely to turn up countless books on programming; this is one field where the resources to teach yourself are highly accessible and available for all levels of competency. Joining a computer club and reading professional magazines are other ways to become more familiar with this career field. In addition, you should start exploring the Internet, itself a great source of information about computer-related careers.

High school and college students who can operate a computer may be able to obtain part-time jobs in business computer centers or in some larger companies. Any computer experience will be helpful for future computer training.

EMPLOYERS

There are approximately 455,000 computer programmers in the United States, and programmers work in locations across the country and in almost every type of business. They work for manufacturing companies, telecommunications companies, data processing service firms, hardware and software companies, banks, insurance companies, credit companies, publishing houses, government agencies, and colleges and universities throughout the country. Many programmers are employed by businesses as consultants on a temporary or contractual basis.

STARTING OUT

You can look for an entry-level programming position in the same way as most other jobs; there is no special or standard point of entry into the field. Individuals with the necessary qualifications should apply directly to companies, agencies, or industries that have announced job openings through a school career services office, an employment agency, or the classified ads.

Students in two- or four-year degree programs should work closely with their schools' career services offices, since major local employers often list job openings exclusively with such offices.

The History of Computing

Visit these Web sites to learn more about the history of computer science and the Internet.

CGI Historical Timeline
http://accad.osu.edu/~waynec/history/timeline.html

Hobbes Internet Timeline
http://www.zakon.org/robert/internet/timeline

IEEE Computer Society History of Computing
http://www.computer.org/portal/pages/ieeecs/education/history.html

Internet Society
http://www.isoc.org/internet/history

Past Notable Women of Computing
http://www.cs.yale.edu/homes/tap/past-women-cs.html

Pioneers of Computing
http://vmoc.museophile.org/pioneers

The Virtual Museum of Computing
http://vmoc.museophile.org

If the market for programmers is particularly tight, you may want to obtain an entry-level job with a large corporation or computer software firm, even if the job does not include programming. As jobs in the programming department open up, current employees in other departments are often the first to know, and they are favored over nonemployees during the interviewing process. Getting a foot in the door in this way has proven to be successful for many programmers.

ADVANCEMENT

Programmers are ranked as junior or senior programmers, according to education, experience, and level of responsibility. After programmers have attained the highest available programming position, they can choose to make one of several career moves in order to be promoted still higher.

Some programmers are more interested in the analysis aspect of computing than in the actual charting and coding of programming.

They often acquire additional training and experience in order to prepare themselves for promotion to positions as systems programmers or *systems analysts*. These individuals have the added responsibility of working with upper management to define equipment and cost guidelines for a specific project. They perform only broad programming tasks, leaving most of the detail work to programmers.

Other programmers become more interested in administration and management and may wish to become heads of programming departments. They tend to be more people oriented and enjoy leading others to excellence. As the level of management responsibilities increases, the amount of technical work performed decreases, so management positions are not for everyone.

Still other programmers may branch out into different technical areas, such as total computer operations, hardware design, and software or network engineering. With experience, they may be placed in charge of the data systems center. They may also decide to go to work for a consulting company, work that generally pays extremely well.

Programming provides a solid background in the computer industry. Experienced programmers enjoy a wide variety of possibilities for career advancement. The hardest part for programmers usually is deciding exactly what they want to do.

EARNINGS

According to the National Association of Colleges and Employers, the average starting salary for college graduates with bachelor's degrees in computer science was $51,070 in 2007. The U.S. Department of Labor reports the median annual salary for computer programmers was $65,510 in 2006. The lowest paid 10 percent of programmers earned less than $38,460 annually, and at the other end of the pay scale, the highest paid 10 percent earned more than $106,610 that same year. Programmers in the West and the Northeast are generally paid more than those in the South and Midwest. This is because most big computer companies are located in the Silicon Valley in California or in the state of Washington, where Microsoft, a major employer of programmers, has its headquarters. Also, some industries, such as public utilities and data processing service firms, tend to pay their programmers higher wages than do other types of employers, such as banks and schools.

Most programmers receive the customary paid vacation and sick leave and are included in such company benefits as group insurance and retirement benefit plans.

WORK ENVIRONMENT

Most programmers work in pleasant office conditions, since computers require an air-conditioned, dust-free environment. Programmers perform most of their duties in one primary location but may be asked to travel to other computing sites on occasion. Because of advances in technology, telecommuting is an increasingly common option for computer professionals, allowing them to work remotely.

The average programmer works between 35 and 40 hours weekly. In some job situations, the programmer may have to work nights or weekends on short notice. This might happen when a program is going through its trial runs, for example, or when there are many demands for additional services. As with other workers who spend long periods in front of a computer terminal typing at a keyboard, programmers are susceptible to eyestrain, back discomfort, and hand and wrist problems, such as carpal tunnel syndrome.

OUTLOOK

Employment for computer programmers is expected to grow more slowly than the average for all occupations through 2014, according to the U.S. Department of Labor. Factors that make job growth for this profession slower than job growth for other computer industry professions include new technologies that eliminate the need for some routine programming work of the past, the increased availability of packaged software programs, the outsourcing of programming jobs overseas, and the increased sophistication of computer users who are able to write and implement their own programs. Jobs should be most plentiful in data processing service firms, software houses, and computer consulting businesses.

According to the U.S. Department of Labor, job applicants with the best chances of employment will be college graduates with strong object-oriented programming capabilities and technical specialization in areas such as wireless applications, multimedia technology, client/server programming, and graphic user interface.

In addition, the best applicants will have some training or experience in an applied field such as accounting, science, engineering, or management. Competition for jobs will be heavier among graduates of two-year data processing programs and among people with equivalent experience or with less training. Since this field is constantly changing, programmers should stay abreast of the latest technology to remain competitive. Growing emphasis on cyber-security will lead to demand for programmers familiar with digital security issues.

FOR MORE INFORMATION

For information on internships, student membership, and the student magazine Crossroads, *contact*
Association for Computing Machinery
1515 Broadway
New York, NY 10036-8901
Tel: 800-342-6626
Email: sigs@acm.org
http://www.acm.org

For information on the Information Technology industry, contact
Association of Information Technology Professionals
401 North Michigan Avenue, Suite 2400
Chicago, IL 60611-4267
Tel: 800-224-9371
http://www.aitp.org

For information on scholarships, student membership, and to read Careers in Computer Science and Computer Engineering, *visit the IEEE's Web site:*
IEEE Computer Society
1730 Massachusetts Avenue, NW
Washington, DC 20036-1992
Tel: 202-371-0101
Email: membership@computer.org
http://www.computer.org

For information on certification programs, contact
Institute for Certification of Computing Professionals
2350 East Devon Avenue, Suite 115
Des Plaines, IL 60018-4610
Tel: 800-843-8227
Email: office@iccp.org
http://www.iccp.org

For information on careers in Information Technology, contact
National Workforce Center for Emerging Technologies
Bellevue Community College
3000 Landerholm Circle, SE, N258
Bellevue, WA 98007-6484
http://www.nwcet.org/programs/cyberCareers/default.asp

Computer Support Service Owners

OVERVIEW

The owners of computer support services help businesses and individuals install and maintain computer hardware and software. They offer advice on what computers to purchase; they teach how to operate computers; and they assist with computer problems as they arise. There are approximately 518,000 computer support specialists in the industry, including technicians and entrepreneurs. *Computer consultants* either work out of their homes, or they rent office space. Though some of their assistance is offered over the phone, much of their work is performed on-site.

HISTORY

Did you know there are museums devoted to "antique" computer hardware? Hang on to those old monitors, keyboards, and hard drives—they may be worth something to collectors and archivists some day. When you think about computers, you are probably not thinking about the past. Computer hardware and software is most often talked about in terms of the future, but computer technology has been in development for over a century. In 1854, George Boole invented Boolean Algebra, a symbol and logic system used as the basis of computer design.

The 1950s brought IBM's first computers and the computer programming languages COBOL and LISP. By the late 1960s, people with computer skills served as consultants to develop hardware and software for manufacturers. The Independent Computer Consultants Association (ICCA) was founded in 1976. Consultants had many more opportunities when even small

QUICK FACTS

School Subjects
Business
Computer science
Technical/shop

Personal Skills
Helping/teaching
Technical/scientific

Work Environment
Primarily indoors
Primarily multiple locations

Minimum Education Level
Associate's degree

Salary Range
$25,290 to $41,470 to
$150,000+

Certification or Licensing
Voluntary

Outlook
Faster than the average

DOT
039

GOE
02.06.01

NOC
2282

O*NET-SOC
15-1041.00

businesses began investing in computers. Office software, such as spreadsheet programs and programs that link computers together with a shared hard drive, were developed in the early 1980s. Many businesses and schools required the regular services of computer support technicians by the late 1980s. Today, computer support service workers play an integral role in the success of businesses large and small.

THE JOB

If your computer's not working, the problem may be simply that you have forgotten to plug in the machine. But it can be much more complicated than that, requiring the assistance of someone with a great deal of computer knowledge. Today's hardware and software are easier to use than in previous years, but can be difficult to install correctly and difficult to learn. Computer support service owners use their computer expertise to help businesses and individuals buy new computers and ready them for daily use.

With their operations based in their home office, computer support service owners take calls from new clients, as well as clients who regularly rely on their services. Clients may have problems with their printers not responding to computer commands; a computer may be locked up; they may have problems performing the particular functions their software is designed for. In some cases, support service owners are able to diagnose the problem and offer assistance over the phone. But in most cases, they are required to go to the offices and work hands-on with the computer systems. Armed with a cell phone, pager, and laptop, they drive to the offices of businesses small and large and the homes of personal computer owners to help get the computers running again. They will install network systems and new hardware and software. They upgrade existing systems. Computer support service owners also teach the computer operators how to use the new systems, either one on one or in group training sessions. They advise on the purchase of hardware and software, and can prepare backup methods.

Many computer consultants also offer their expertise in Web design and multimedia for uploading a Web page, preparing a presentation, and offering desktop publishing services. They also help to create computer databases. Some computer consultants are involved in issues of programming.

Brad Crotteau started his own computer support service in 1991, and his business has grown into Crocker Networking Solutions Inc. He anticipated that some of the demands of the job would become more difficult as he got older, so he recently made some decisions about the nature of his business. "I knew I didn't always want to be crawling around, plugging computers in," he says. So Crotteau incorporated his business and took on a staff of nine employees, including technicians, sales people, administrative assistants, trainers, and Web designers.

Crotteau's day starts early at 7:00 A.M. with paperwork, followed at around 8:00 A.M. by phone calls from businesses. He then must work the new requests for service into his daily schedule. Though he has a staff of nine, Crotteau is still actively involved in the technical work of installing systems and troubleshooting, and the generating of estimates and other financial details. He makes it a point to end his workday at 6:00 P.M., though he is required to work some overtime. "I have stayed up until 4:00 A.M.," he says, "bringing a service up for a client, but that's rare." His client base consists of businesses with between five and 85 personal computers. The biggest challenge can be correcting user-generated problems. Crotteau says giving an inexperienced computer user a complex system "is like giving a Maserati to someone who just started riding horses a few weeks ago."

Crotteau's support service is also embarking on a new business venture. He has trademarked many of his company's services, and now offers them as a product called "Performance Net." His company sells the network systems, and then puts the systems into place. This venture has been helped along by a business alliance with a manufacturer of software. Crotteau's company has been hired by the manufacturer to install their servers in businesses all across the country.

In addition to technical work, the owners of computer support services must handle all the details of running their businesses. They handle phone calls, bookkeeping, and client records. They must also research new technologies and keep up to date on advanced technical skills. Maintaining connections within the industry is also important; computer support system owners may need to call upon the assistance of other consultants and technicians to help with some projects.

REQUIREMENTS
High School
Of course, you should take any classes that will familiarize you with computers. Computer science classes will help you learn about operating systems and programming. Learn about the various software, like word processing and spreadsheet programs, as well as the languages of Web page design. Taking a journalism class and working on your school newspaper will involve you with multimedia presentation and teach you about page layout and graphic design. Take courses in business and accounting to prepare for the bookkeeping and

administrative details of the work. English composition and communication courses can help you develop teaching skills.

Postsecondary Training

Though a degree is not required for you to start your own computer support service, most service owners and consultants have at least an associate's degree. Some consultants supplement their education with special training offered by computer software companies such as Novell and Microsoft. Many consultants registered with the ICCA have advanced degrees and highly technical training in such areas as robotics, telecommunications, and nuclear engineering. Community colleges and universities across the country have programs in computer science, computer engineering, and electrical engineering. For a degree in computer science, you will be required to take courses in calculus, English composition, program design, algorithms, computer graphics, and database management. Electrical engineering programs include courses in BASIC programming, industrial electronics, digital integrated circuits, and microprocessor systems. In addition to seminars, you will also attend labs. Some bachelor's programs include research projects in which you will work closely with a faculty member to study new technologies. Some software companies offer training programs.

Very few consultants start their own businesses straight out of college. Some years working full-time as part of a computer service staff will give you the firsthand experience you will need. Not only will you develop your computer expertise, but you will learn what is required in operating a business.

Certification or Licensing

There are many different kinds of certifications available to people working in computer support and consulting. No one certification, however, serves all the varying needs of computer professionals. Some consultants get certified in database design and administration. Some consultants have Microsoft certified system engineer (MCSE) status. Visit http://www.microsoft.com/learning/mcp/mcse for information on the MCSE exam, which tests your understanding of Windows networks, hardware requirements and installations, and system maintenance. This certification should only supplement an extensive computer background, not replace it. The term "paper MCSE" has evolved in the industry to describe those who "look good on paper" with their certification, but do not have the networking and computer science education and experience to back it up.

The Institute for Certification of Computer Professionals offers a certified computer professional exam. Nearly 55,000 computer professionals hold the certification, having passed an exam that tests knowledge of business information systems, data resource management, software engineering, and other subjects.

Other Requirements

You should have good business and money management skills. Though some months you may have more work than you can handle, with a steady flow of income, other months there may be no work at all. You will have to budget your money to carry you through the lean months. Computer skills are very important, but you will also need good people skills to maintain customer relations.

Teaching skills are important, because you will be training people in how to use their systems. "You need the ability to talk to people in a language they can understand," Brad Crotteau says, "but don't talk down to them. You have to gauge your client's understanding."

EXPLORING

Get to know your own home computer—study the software and its manuals, and familiarize yourself with computer programming languages. Read some of the many magazines devoted to computers, such as *MacWorld* (http://www.macworld.com). Find out who services the computers in your school, and ask to spend some time with the technicians. But do not just focus on the technical duties of the people who own computer support services; find out how they go about running an office and maintaining a small business. Join your school's business club and you'll have the opportunity to meet small business owners in your area.

EMPLOYERS

Approximately 518,000 computer support specialists are employed in the United States. Computer support service owners work for a variety of different clients, servicing the personal computers in home-based offices, as well as contracting with large companies for long-term assistance. Though many individuals have computers in their homes for their personal use, few of them seek out professional service. The main clients of support service owners will be accounting firms, insurance agencies, government departments— any business or organization that relies upon computers to perform daily operations. Even a company that has its own full-time support staff will occasionally hire outside consultants. Computer support services are in demand all across the country, but are most successful in large cities, as they can draw from a broader client base.

STARTING OUT

Brad Crotteau had been working for Pacific Gas and Electric as an engineer for 14 years when he began developing his own business on the side. "The main concern for people starting their own businesses," Crotteau says, "is how they're going to capitalize their company." Brad was fortunate to receive an early retirement package, and then worked for a while as a computer consultant for a private consulting company. Once he'd felt he'd gotten his feet wet, he was ready to start full time with his own support service. "You should work for a large corporation," Crotteau advises, "to learn about human resources, compensation packages, benefits. You need to develop a good business sense. That's why many small businesses fail; you may be great at computers, but bad at business."

As with many start-ups, it's good for you to focus your talents. Decide on a niche such as networking or package customization; then promote those specific services. Crotteau credits much of his success to good marketing techniques, which includes careful attention to image. "You can't do this from the back of your car," he says, "but promoting a good image doesn't have to be expensive. Our biggest sales tool is our business cards. We have a nice, multicolored business card that reads well."

ADVANCEMENT

Once they are established in their niche market, support service owners can expand to include other services. Some computer support services are able to offer much more than technical assistance; they also hold training sessions, prepare multimedia reports and presentations, and design Web pages. The more business connections a support service owner can make with support services, computer manufacturers, and other companies, the better they'll be able to build their client base. As their business grows, support service owners can hire staff to deal with administrative duties, as well as technicians to assist with servicing their clients' computers.

EARNINGS

According to the U.S. Department of Labor, median hourly wages for computer support specialists were $19.94 in 2006, which, based on a 40-hour workweek, is a salary of $41,470 a year. Salaries ranged from less than $25,290 to $68,540 or more annually. Those working in large cities like New York and Los Angeles average more than those in the Midwest, the Southwest, and the Northwest. Someone in New York with more than 10 years experience can average over $90,000 a year, while a consultant with similar experience in the Southwest may make closer to $65,000 a year. Some very experienced, business-minded consultants can make $150,000 a year or more.

WORK ENVIRONMENT

Most computer support businesses are based in a home office or a rented commercial space. Computer support service owners devote a lot of time to sitting at their own computer, managing their accounts and records, but the majority of their time will be in the offices of their clients. In either setting, the work environment will likely be quiet and well lit. The work will be indoors, though support service owners will travel from office to office throughout the day.

When installing and repairing computer hardware, support service owners may have to crawl around behind desks to hook up wires and plug in cords. This work is essentially unsupervised, but some clients may ask to receive instruction and information about the repairs being made. In some cases, support service owners may work as part of a team, particularly if they are brought into a large company with a full-time support staff.

Some consultants work much more than 40 hours a week, though support service owners can avoid this by developing strong business management skills. "If you're working 80 hours a week," Brad Crotteau says, "something's wrong. You'll have to work hard, but you don't have to obsess about it."

OUTLOOK

According to the U.S. Department of Labor, the industry is expected to grow quickly as computer systems become more important to many businesses. Lower prices on computer hardware and software will inspire businesses to expand their systems, and to invest in the services needed to keep them up and running. As computer programs become more sophisticated and are able to perform more complex operations, consultants will be needed to help clients operate these programs. With companies relying more on complex computer systems, they will be less likely to take risks in the installation of hardware and software. To stay at the top of the industry, consultants will have to keep up on technological developments and take continuing education courses.

More consultants may also become involved in broadening computer literacy. Computer resources are generally limited to middle-class students; some nonprofit organizations are forming to bring more computers and support services to inner-city youth, low-income families, and people with disabilities.

FOR MORE INFORMATION

To learn more about membership and career training seminars, contact
Association of Computer Support Specialists
333 Mamaroneck Avenue, #129
White Plains, NY 10605-1440
http://www.acss.org

To learn about membership benefits, contact
Independent Computer Consultants Association
11131 South Towne Square, Suite F
St. Louis, MO 63123-7817
Tel: 800-774-4222
Email: info@icca.org
http://www.icca.org

For information on certification programs, contact
Institute for Certification of Computing Professionals
2350 East Devon Avenue, Suite 115
Des Plaines, IL 60018-4610
Tel: 800-843-8227
Email: office@iccp.org
http://www.iccp.org

For resume and cover letter advice, salary statistics, and other career information in information technology, visit
Robert Half Technology
http://www.roberthalftechnology.com

Computer Support Specialists

OVERVIEW

Computer support specialists investigate and resolve problems in computer functioning. They listen to customer complaints, walk customers through possible solutions, and write technical reports based on their work. Computer support specialists have different duties depending on whom they assist and what they fix. Regardless of specialty, all computer support specialists must be very knowledgeable about the products with which they work and be able to communicate effectively with users from different technical backgrounds. They must be patient and professional with frustrated users and be able to perform well under stress. Computer support is similar to solving mysteries, so support specialists should enjoy the challenge of problem solving and have strong analytical skills. There are approximately 518,000 computer support specialists employed in the United States.

HISTORY

The first major advances in modern computer technology were made during World War II. After the war, it was thought that the enormous size of computers, which easily took up the space of entire warehouses, would limit their use to huge government projects. The 1950 census, for example, was computer-processed.

The introduction of semiconductors to computer technology made possible smaller and less expensive computers. Businesses began adapting computers to their operations as early as 1954. Within 30 years, computers had revolutionized the way people work, play,

QUICK FACTS

School Subjects
Computer science
English
Mathematics

Personal Skills
Helping/teaching
Technical/scientific

Work Environment
Primarily indoors
Primarily one location

Minimum Education Level
Some postsecondary training

Salary Range
$25,290 to $41,470 to
$68,540+

Certification or Licensing
Recommended

Outlook
Faster than the average

DOT
033

GOE
02.06.01

NOC
6221

O*NET-SOC
15-1041.00

and shop. Today, computers are everywhere, from businesses of all kinds to government agencies, charitable organizations, and private homes. Over the years, technology has continued to shrink computer size and increase speed at an unprecedented rate.

Computer support has been around since the development of the first computers for the simple reason that, like all machines, computers experience problems at one time or another. Several market phenomena explain the increase in demand for competent computer support specialists. First of all, as more and more companies enter the computer hardware, software, and peripheral market, the intense competition to win customers has resulted in many companies offering free or reasonably priced technical support as part of the purchase package. A company uses its reputation and the availability of a computer support department to differentiate its products from those of other companies, even though the tangible products like a hard drive, for example, may actually be physically identical. Second, personal computers have entered private homes in large numbers, and the sheer quantity of users has risen so dramatically that more technical support specialists are needed to field their complaints. Third, technological advances hit the marketplace in the form of a new processor or software application so quickly that quality assurance departments cannot possibly identify all the glitches in programming beforehand. Finally, given the great variety of computer equipment and software on the market, it is often difficult for users to reach a high proficiency level with each individual program. When they experience problems, often due to their own errors, users call on computer support to help them. The goal of many computer companies is to release a product for sale that requires no computer support, so that the computer support department has nothing to do. Given the speed of development, however, this is not likely to occur anytime soon. Until it does, there will be a strong demand for computer support specialists. A growing tendency among companies to outsource computer support jobs overseas will dampen job growth in the United States.

THE JOB

It is relatively rare today to find a business that does not rely on computers for at least something. Some use them heavily and in many areas: daily operations, such as employee time clocks; monthly projects, such as payroll and sales accounting; and major reengineering of fundamental business procedures, such as form automation in government agencies, insurance companies, and banks. As more companies become reliant on computers, it becomes increasingly critical that they function properly all the time. Any computer down-

Computer support specialists at a Dell customer contact center help callers troubleshoot problems with their computers. *(AP Images)*

time can be extremely expensive, in terms of work left undone and sales not made, for example. When employees experience problems with their computer system, they call computer support for help. Computer support specialists investigate and resolve problems in computer functioning.

Computer support can generally be broken up into at least three distinct areas, although these distinctions vary greatly with the nature, size, and scope of the company. The three most prevalent areas are user support, technical support, and microcomputer support. Most computer support specialists perform some combination of the tasks explained below.

The jobs of computer support specialists vary according to whom they assist and what they fix. Some specialists help private users exclusively; others are on call to a major corporate buyer. Some work with computer hardware and software, while others help with printer, modem, and fax problems. *User support specialists*, also known as *help desk specialists*, work directly with users themselves, who call when they experience problems. The support specialist listens carefully to the user's explanation of the precise nature of the problem and the commands entered that seem to have caused it. Some companies have developed complex software that allows the support specialist to enter a description of the problem and wait for the computer to provide suggestions about what the user should do.

The initial goal is to isolate the source of the problem. If user error is the culprit, the user support specialist explains procedures related to the program in question, whether it is a graphics, database, word processing, or printing program. If the problem seems to lie in the hardware or software, the specialist asks the user to enter certain commands in order to see if the computer makes the appropriate response. If it does not, the support specialist is closer to isolating the cause. The support specialist consults supervisors, programmers, and others in order to outline the cause and possible solutions.

Some *technical support specialists* who work for computer companies are mainly involved with solving problems whose cause has been determined to lie in the computer system's operating system, hardware, or software. They make exhaustive use of resources, such as colleagues or books, and try to solve the problem through a variety of methods, including program modifications and the replacement of certain hardware or software.

Technical support specialists employed in the information systems departments of large corporations do this kind of troubleshooting as well. They also oversee the daily operations of the various computer systems in the company. Sometimes they compare the system's work capacity to the actual daily workload in order to determine if upgrades are needed. In addition, they might help out other computer professionals in the company with modifying commercial software for their company's particular needs.

Microcomputer support specialists are responsible for preparing computers for delivery to a client, including installing the operating system and desired software. After the unit is installed at the customer's location, the support specialists might help train users on appropriate procedures and answer any questions they have. They help diagnose problems that occur, transferring major concerns to other support specialists.

All computer support work must be well documented. Support specialists write detailed technical reports on every problem they work on. They try to tie together different problems on the same software, so programmers can make adjustments that address all of the issues. Record keeping is crucial because designers, programmers, and engineers use technical support reports to revise current products and improve future ones. Some support specialists help write training manuals. They are often required to read trade magazines and company newsletters in order to keep up to date on their products and the field in general.

REQUIREMENTS

High School

A high school diploma is a minimum requirement for computer support specialists. Any technical courses you can take, such as computer science, schematic drawing, or electronics, can help you develop the logical and analytical thinking skills necessary to be successful in this field. Courses in math and science are also valuable for this reason. Since computer support specialists have to deal with both computer programmers on the one hand and computer users who may not know anything about computers on the other, you should take English and speech classes to improve your verbal and written communications skills.

Postsecondary Training

Computer support is a field as old as computer technology itself, so it might seem odd that postsecondary programs in this field are not more common or standardized. The reason behind this situation is relatively simple: Formal education curricula cannot keep up with the changes, nor can they provide specific training on individual products. Some large corporations might consider educational background, both as a way to weed out applicants and to insure a certain level of proficiency. Most major computer companies, however, look for energetic individuals who demonstrate a willingness and ability to learn new things quickly and who have general computer knowledge. These employers count on training new support specialists themselves.

Individuals interested in pursuing a job in this field should first determine what area of computer support appeals to them the most and then honestly assess their level of experience and knowledge. Large corporations often prefer to hire people with an associate's degree and some experience. They may also be impressed with commercial certification in a computer field, such as networking. However, if they are hiring from within the company, they will probably weigh experience more heavily than education when making a final decision.

Employed individuals looking for a career change may want to commit themselves to a program of self-study in order to be qualified for computer support positions. Many computer professionals learn a lot of what they know by playing around on computers, reading trade magazines, and talking with colleagues. Self-taught individuals should learn how to effectively demonstrate their knowledge and proficiency on the job or during an interview. Besides self-training, employed individuals should investigate tuition reimbursement programs offered by their company.

High school students with no experience should seriously consider earning an associate's degree in a computer-related technology. The degree shows the prospective employer that the applicant has attained a certain level of proficiency with computers and has the intellectual ability to learn technical processes, a promising sign for success on the job.

Many computer technology programs lead to an associate's degree. A specialization in personal computer support and administration is certainly applicable to technical support. Most computer professionals eventually need to go back to school to earn a bachelor's degree in order to keep themselves competitive in the job market and prepare themselves for promotion to other computer fields.

Certification or Licensing

Though certification is not an industry requirement, it is highly recommended. According to HDI, a professional association for computer support specialists, most individuals wishing to qualify to work in a support/help desk environment will need to obtain certification within a month of being on the job. A number of organizations offer several different types of certification. CompTIA: The Computing Technology Industry Association, for example, offers the "A+" certification for entry-level computer service technicians. HDI has training courses and offers a number of certifications for those working in support and help desk positions.

To become certified, you will need to pass a written test and in some cases may need a certain amount of work experience. Although going through the certification process is voluntary, becoming certified will most likely be to your advantage. It will show your commitment to the profession as well as demonstrate your level of expertise. In addition, certification may qualify you for certain jobs and lead to new employment opportunities.

Other Requirements

To be a successful computer support specialist, you should be patient, enjoy challenges of problem solving, and think logically. You should work well under stress and demonstrate effective communication skills. Working in a field that changes rapidly, you should be naturally curious and enthusiastic about learning new technologies as they are developed.

EXPLORING

If you are interested in becoming a computer support specialist, you should try to organize a career day with an employed computer support specialist. Local computer repair shops that offer computer support service might be a good place to contact. Otherwise, you should contact major corporations, computer companies, and even the central office of your school system.

If you are interested in any computer field, you should start working and playing on computers as much as possible; many working computer professionals became computer hobbyists at a very young age. You can surf the Internet, read computer magazines, and join school or community computer clubs.

You might also attend a computer technology course at a local technical/vocational school. This would give you hands-on exposure to typical computer support training. In addition, if you experience problems with your own hardware or software, you should call computer support, paying careful attention to how the support specialist handles the call and asking as many questions as the specialist has time to answer.

EMPLOYERS

Computer support specialists work for computer hardware and software companies, as well as in the information systems departments of large corporations and government agencies. There are approximately 518,000 computer support specialists employed in the United States.

STARTING OUT

Most computer support positions are considered entry-level. They are found mainly in computer companies and large corporations. Individuals interested in obtaining a job in this field should scan the classified ads for openings in local businesses and may want to work with an employment agency for help finding out about opportunities. Since many job openings are publicized by word of mouth, it is also very important to speak with as many working computer professionals as possible. They tend to be aware of job openings before anyone else and may be able to offer a recommendation to the hiring committee.

If students of computer technology are seeking a position in computer support, they should work closely with their school's career services office. Many employers inform career services offices at nearby schools of openings before ads are run in the newspaper. In addition, career services office staffs are generally very helpful with resume writing assistance and interviewing techniques.

If an employee wants to make a career change into computer support, he or she should contact the human resources department of the company or speak directly with appropriate management. In companies that are expanding their computing systems, it is often helpful for management to know that current employees would be interested in growing in a computer-related direction. They may even be willing to finance additional education.

ADVANCEMENT

Computer support specialists who demonstrate leadership skills and a strong aptitude for the work may be promoted to supervisory positions within computer support departments. Supervisors are responsible for the more complicated problems that arise, as well as for some administrative duties such as scheduling, interviewing, and job assignments.

Further promotion requires additional education. Some computer support specialists may become commercially certified in computer networking so that they can install, maintain, and repair computer networks. Others may prefer to pursue a bachelor's degree in computer science, either full time or part time. The range of careers available to college graduates varies widely. *Software engineers* analyze industrial, business, and scientific problems and develop software programs to handle them effectively. *Quality assurance engineers* design automated quality assurance tests for new software applications. *Internet quality assurance* specialists work specifically with testing and developing companies' Web sites. *Computer systems programmer-analysts* study the broad computing picture for a company or a group of companies in order to determine the best way to organize the computer systems.

There are limited opportunities for computer support specialists to be promoted into managerial positions. Doing so would require additional education in business but would probably also depend on the individual's advanced computer knowledge.

EARNINGS

Computer support specialist jobs are plentiful in areas where clusters of computer companies are located, such as northern California and Seattle, Washington. Median annual earnings for computer support specialists were $41,470 in 2006, according to the U.S. Department of Labor. The highest 10 percent earned more than $68,540, while the lowest 10 percent earned less than $25,290. Those who have more education, responsibility, and expertise have the potential to earn much more.

Computer support specialists earned the following mean annual salaries by industry in 2006 (according to the U.S. Department of Labor): software publishers; $51,180; computer systems design and related services, $46,020; colleges and universities, $41,450; and elementary and secondary schools, $39,810.

Most computer support specialists work for companies that offer a full range of benefits, including health insurance, paid vacation, and sick leave. Smaller service or start-up companies may hire support specialists on a contractual basis.

WORK ENVIRONMENT

Computer support specialists work in comfortable business environments. They generally work regular, 40-hour weeks. For certain products, however, they may be asked to work evenings or weekends or at least be on call during those times in case of emergencies. If they work for service companies, they may be required to travel to clients' sites and log overtime hours.

Computer support work can be stressful, since specialists often deal with frustrated users who may be difficult to work with. Communication problems with people who are less technically qualified may also be a source of frustration. Patience and understanding are essential for handling these problems.

Computer support specialists are expected to work quickly and efficiently and be able to perform under pressure. The ability to do this requires thorough technical expertise and keen analytical ability.

OUTLOOK

The U.S. Department of Labor predicts that employment for computer support specialists will grow faster than the average for all occupations through 2014. Each time a new computer product is released on the market or another system is installed, there will be problems, whether from user error or technical difficulty. Therefore, there will always be a need for computer support specialists to solve the problems. Since technology changes so rapidly, it is very important for these professionals to keep up to date on advances. They should read trade magazines, surf the Internet, and talk with colleagues in order to know what is happening in the field. Job growth will be weaker than growth during the previous decade as many computer support jobs are being outsourced overseas.

Since some companies stop offering computer support on old products or applications after a designated time, the key is to be flexible with your understanding of technology. This is important for another reason as well. While the industry as a whole will require more computer support specialists in the future, it may be the case that certain computer companies go out of business. It can be a volatile industry for start-ups or young companies dedicated to the development of one product. Computer support specialists interested in working for computer companies should therefore consider living in areas in which many such companies are clustered. In this way, it will be easier to find another job if necessary.

FOR MORE INFORMATION

For information on internships, scholarships, student membership, and the student magazine Crossroads, *contact*
Association for Computing Machinery
2 Penn Plaza, Suite 701
New York, NY 10121-0701
Tel: 800-342-6626
Email: acmhelp@acm.org
http://www.acm.org

To learn more about membership and career training seminars, contact
Association of Computer Support Specialists
333 Mamaroneck Avenue, #129
White Plains, NY 10605-1440
http://www.acss.org

For information on certification, contact
CompTIA: The Computing Technology Industry Association
1815 South Meyers Road, Suite 300
Oakbrook Terrace, IL 60181-5228
Tel: 630-678-8300
http://www.comptia.org

For more information on this organization's training courses and certification, contact
HDI
102 South Tejon, Suite 1200
Colorado Springs, CO 80903-2231
Tel: 800-248-5667
Email: support@thinkhdi.com
http://www.thinkhdi.com

For information on scholarships, student membership, and to read Careers in Computer Science and Computer Engineering, *visit IEEE's Web site:*
IEEE Computer Society
1730 Massachusetts Avenue, NW
Washington, DC 20036-1992
Tel: 202-371-0101
Email: membership@computer.org
http://www.computer.org

Computer Systems Programmer-Analysts

QUICK FACTS

School Subjects
Computer science
Mathematics

Personal Skills
Mechanical/manipulative
Technical/scientific

Work Environment
Primarily indoors
Primarily one location

Minimum Education Level
Bachelor's degree

Salary Range
$42,780 to $69,760 to
$106,820+

Certification or Licensing
Voluntary

Outlook
Much faster than the average

DOT
033

GOE
02.06.01

NOC
2162

O*NET-SOC
15-1051.00

OVERVIEW

Computer systems programmer-analysts analyze the computing needs of a business and then design a new system or upgrade an old system to meet those needs. The position can be split between two people, the *systems programmer* and the *systems analyst*, but it is frequently held by just one person, who oversees the work from beginning to end.

HISTORY

The first major advances in modern computer technology were made during World War II. After the war, people thought that computers were too big (they easily filled entire warehouses) to ever be used for anything other than government projects, such as the processing of the 1950 census.

The introduction of semiconductors to computer technology led to the creation of smaller and less expensive computers. The semiconductors replaced the bigger, slower vacuum tubes of the first computers. These changes made it easier for businesses to adapt computers to their needs, which they began doing as early as 1954. Within 30 years, computers had revolutionized the way people work, play, and even shop. Today, computers are everywhere, from businesses of all kinds to government agencies, charitable organizations, and private homes. Over the years, technology has continued to shrink computer size and increase operating speeds at an unprecedented rate.

The need for systems programmer-analysts grew out of the proliferation of hardware and software products on the market. While many offices have an unofficial "computer expert," whose main job may be in accounting, word processing, or office administration, most medium-size to larger companies that have invested in expensive computer systems have found the need to employ, either full time or on a consulting basis, a systems analyst or programmer-analyst.

In addition, the computer revolution brought with it awareness that choosing the appropriate system from the start is crucial to business success. Purchasing decisions are based on many complicated scientific and mathematical models as well as on practical business sense. Therefore, systems analysts have become essential to business decision-making.

Businesses and organizations also discovered that, like all new technology, computer systems break down a lot. It has become more cost effective for many organizations to have full-time systems analysts on site instead of calling computer repairers to fix every small glitch.

THE JOB

Businesses invest hundreds of thousands of dollars in computer systems to make their operations more efficient and thus, more profitable. As older systems become obsolete, businesses are also faced with the task of replacing or upgrading them with new technology. Computer systems programmer-analysts plan and develop new computer systems or upgrade existing systems to meet changing business needs. They also install, modify, and maintain functioning computer systems. The process of choosing and implementing a computer system is similar for programmer-analysts who work for very different employers. However, specific decisions in terms of hardware and software differ depending on the industry.

The first stage of the process involves meeting with management and users in order to discuss the problem at hand. For example, a company's accounting system might be slow, unreliable, and generally outdated. During many hours of meetings, systems programmer-analysts and management discuss various options, including commercial software, hardware upgrades, and customizing possibilities that may solve the problems. At the end of the discussions, which may last as long as several weeks or months, the programmer-analyst defines the specific system goals as agreed upon by participants.

Next, systems programmer-analysts engage in highly analytic and logical activities. They use tools such as structural analysis, data modeling, mathematics, and cost accounting to determine which computers, including hardware and software and peripherals, will be required to meet the goals of the project. They must consider the trade-offs between extra efficiency and speed and increased costs. Weighing the pros and cons of each additional system feature is an important factor in system planning. Whatever preliminary decisions are made must be supported by mathematical and financial evidence.

As the final stage of the planning process, systems programmer-analysts prepare reports and formal presentations to be delivered to management. Reports must be written in clear, concise language that business professionals, who are not necessarily technical experts, can understand thoroughly. Formal presentations in front of groups of various sizes are often required as part of the system proposal.

If the system or the system upgrades are approved, equipment is purchased and installed. Then, the programmer-analysts get down to the real technical work so that all the different computers and peripherals function well together. They prepare specifications, diagrams, and other programming structures and, often using computer-aided systems engineering (CASE) technology, they write the new or upgraded programming code. If they work solely as systems analysts, it is at this point that they hand over all of their information to the systems programmer so that he or she can begin to write the programming code.

Systems design and programming involves defining the files and records to be accessed by the system, outlining the processing steps, and suggesting formats for output that meet the needs of the company. User-friendliness of the front-end applications is extremely important for user productivity. Therefore, programmer-analysts must be able to envision how nontechnical system users view their on-screen work. Systems programmer-analysts might also specify security programs that allow only authorized personnel access to certain files or groups of files.

As the programs are written, programmer-analysts set up test runs of various parts of the system, making sure each step of the way that major goals are reached. Once the system is up and running, problems, or "bugs," begin to pop up. Programmer-analysts are responsible for fixing these last-minute problems. They must isolate the problem and review the hundreds of lines of programming commands to determine where the mistake is located. Then they must enter the correct command or code and recheck the program.

Depending on the employer, some systems programmer-analysts might be involved with computer networking. Network communication programs tell two or more computers or peripherals how to work with each other. When a system is composed of equipment from various manufacturers, networking is essential for smooth

Mean Annual Earnings by Specialty, 2006

Computer and peripheral equipment manufacturing	$86,900
Scientific research and development services	$85,390
Professional and commercial equipment and supplies	$82,890
Securities and commodity contracts intermediation	$81,980
Internet publishing and broadcasting	$81,390
Computer systems design and related services	$74,800
Management of companies and enterprises	$72,250
Insurance carriers	$71,170
State government	$61,000

Source: U.S. Department of Labor

system functioning. For example, shared printers have to know how to order print jobs as they come in from various terminals. Some programmer-analysts write the code that establishes printing queues. Others might be involved in user training, since they know the software applications well. They might also customize commercial software programs to meet the needs of their company.

Many programmer-analysts become specialized in an area of business, science, or engineering. They seek education and further on-the-job training in these areas to develop expertise. They may therefore attend special seminars, workshops, and classes designed for their needs. This extra knowledge allows them to develop a deeper understanding of the computing problems specific to the business or industry.

REQUIREMENTS
High School
Take a college preparatory program with advanced classes in math, science, and computer science to prepare you for this work. This will provide a foundation of basic concepts and encourage the development of analytic and logical thinking skills. Since programmer-analysts do a lot of proposal writing that may or may not be technical in nature, English classes are valuable as well. Speech classes will help prepare you for making formal presentations to management and clients.

Postsecondary Training

A bachelor's degree in computer science, information science, or management information systems is a minimum requirement for systems programmer-analysts. Course work in preparation for this field includes math, computer programming, science, and logic. Several years of related work experience, including knowledge of programming languages, are often necessary as well. For some very high-level positions, an advanced degree in a specific computer subfield may be required. As a result of the rapid growth of electronic commerce, some firms are also seeking analysts with a master's degree in business administration, with a concentration in information systems. Also, depending on the employer, proficiency in business, science, or engineering may be necessary.

Certification or Licensing

Some programmer-analysts pursue certification through the Institute for Certification of Computing Professionals. In particular, they take classes and exams to become certified computing professionals (CCPs). Others pursue the information systems analyst designation, which requires applicants to complete a four-year undergraduate information systems degree program and pass an examination. Certification is voluntary and is an added credential for job hunters. Certification demonstrates to employers that applicants have achieved a recognized level of knowledge and experience in principles and practices related to systems.

Other Requirements

Successful systems programmer-analysts demonstrate strong analytic skills and enjoy the challenges of problem solving. They are able to understand problems that exist on many levels, from technical to practical to business oriented. They can visualize complicated and abstract relationships between computer hardware and software and are good at matching needs to equipment.

Systems programmer-analysts have to be flexible as well. They routinely deal with many different kinds of people, from management to data entry clerks. Therefore, they must be knowledgeable in a lot of functional areas of the company. They should be able to talk to management about cost-effective solutions, to programmers about detailed coding, and to clerks about user-friendliness of the applications.

As is true for all computer professionals, systems programmer-analysts must be able to learn about new technology quickly. They should be naturally curious about keeping up on cutting-edge developments, which can be time consuming. Furthermore, they are often so busy at their jobs that staying in the know is done largely on their own time.

EXPLORING

You have several options to learn more about what it is like to be a computer systems programmer-analyst. You can spend a day with a working professional in this field in order to experience a typical day firsthand. Career days of this type can usually be arranged through school guidance counselors or the public relations manager of local corporations.

Strategy games, such as chess, played with friends or school clubs are a good way to put your analytic thinking skills to use while having fun. When choosing a game, the key is to make sure it relies on qualities similar to those used by programmer-analysts.

Lastly, you should become a computer hobbyist and learn everything you can about computers by working and playing with them on a daily basis. Surfing the Internet regularly, as well as reading trade magazines, will also be helpful. You might also want to try hooking up a mini-system at home or school, configuring terminals, printers, modems, and other peripherals into a coherent system. This activity requires a fair amount of knowledge and should be supervised by a professional.

EMPLOYERS

Computer systems programmer-analysts work for all types of firms and organizations that do their work on computers. Such companies may include manufacturing companies, data processing service firms, hardware and software companies, banks, insurance companies, credit companies, publishing houses, government agencies, financial institutions, Internet service providers, and colleges and universities. Many programmer-analysts are employed by businesses as consultants on a temporary or contractual basis.

STARTING OUT

Since systems programmer-analysts typically have at least some experience in a computer-related job, most are hired into these jobs from lower-level positions within the same company. For example, programmers, software engineering technicians, and network and database administrators all gain valuable computing experience that can be put to good use at a systems job. Alternatively, individuals who acquire expertise in systems programming and analysis while in other jobs may want to work with a headhunter to find the right systems positions for them. Also, trade magazines, newspapers, and employment agencies regularly feature job openings in this field.

Students in four-year degree programs should work closely with their schools' career services offices. Companies regularly work through such offices in order to find the most qualified graduates. Since it may be difficult to find a job as a programmer-analyst to begin with, it is important for students to consider their long-term potential within a certain company. The chance for promotion into a systems job can make lower-level jobs more appealing, at least in the short run.

For those individuals already employed in a computer-related job but wanting to get into systems programming and analysis, additional formal education is a good idea. Some employers have educational reimbursement policies that allow employees to take courses inexpensively. If the employee's training could directly benefit the business, companies are more willing to pay for the expense.

ADVANCEMENT

Systems programmer-analysts already occupy a relatively high-level technical job. Promotion, therefore, usually occurs in one of two directions. First, programmer-analysts can be put in charge of increasingly larger and more complex systems. Instead of concentrating on a company's local system, for example, an analyst can oversee all company systems and networks. This kind of technically based promotion can also put systems programmer-analysts into other areas of computing. With the proper experience and additional training, they can get into database or network management and design, software engineering, or even quality assurance.

The other direction in which programmer-analysts can go is managerial. Depending on the position sought, formal education (either a bachelor's degree in business or a master's in business administration) may be required. As more administrative duties are added, more technical ones are taken away. Therefore, programmer-analysts who enjoy the technical aspect of their work more than anything else may not want to pursue this advancement track. Excellent computing managers have both a solid background in various forms of computing and a good grasp of what it takes to run a department. Also, having the vision to see how technology will change in the short and long terms, and how those changes will affect the industry concerned, is a quality of a good manager.

EARNINGS

According to the U.S. Department of Labor, the median annual salary for computer systems analysts was $69,760 in 2006. At the low end of the pay range, 10 percent of systems analysts earned less than $42,780. The top 10 percent earned $106,820 or more. Salaries are slightly higher in geographic areas where many computer companies are clustered, such as Silicon Valley in California and Seattle,

Washington. The National Association of Colleges and Employers reports that starting salaries for those with a bachelor's degree in computer science averaged $53,396. Those with a bachelor's degree in information sciences and systems averaged $50,852.

Those in senior positions can earn much higher salaries. *Computerworld* reports that senior systems analysts earned a national average of $83,390 in 2006.

Most programmer-analysts receive health insurance, paid vacation, and sick leave. Some employers offer tuition reimbursement programs and in-house computer training workshops.

WORK ENVIRONMENT

Computer systems programmer-analysts work in comfortable office environments. If they work as consultants, they may travel frequently. Otherwise, travel is limited to trade shows, seminars, and visitations to vendors for demonstrations. They might also visit other businesses to observe their systems in action.

Programmer-analysts usually work 40-hour weeks and enjoy the regular holiday schedule of days off. However, as deadlines for system installation, upgrades, and spot-checking approach, they are often required to work overtime. Extra compensation for overtime hours may come in the form of time-and-a-half pay or compensatory time off, depending on the precise nature of the employee's duties, company policy, and state law. If the employer operates off-shifts, programmer-analysts may be on-call to address any problems that might arise at any time of the day or night. This is relatively rare in the service sector but more common in manufacturing, heavy industry, and data processing firms.

Computer systems programming and analysis is very detailed work. The smallest error can cause major system disruptions, which can be a great source of frustration. Systems programmer-analysts must be prepared to deal with this frustration and be able to work well under pressure.

OUTLOOK

Employment for computer systems programmer-analysts will grow much faster than the average for all occupations through 2014. Increases are mainly a product of the growing number of businesses that rely extensively on computers. When businesses automate, their daily operations depend on the capacity of their computer systems to perform at desired levels. The continuous development of new technologies means that businesses must also update their old systems to remain competitive in the marketplace. Additionally, the need for businesses to network their information adds to the demand for qualified programmer-analysts. Businesses will rely increasingly on systems programmer-analysts to make the right purchasing decisions and to keep systems running smoothly.

Many computer manufacturers are beginning to expand the range of services they offer to business clients. In the years to come, they may hire many systems programmer-analysts to work as consultants on a per-project basis with a potential client. These workers would perform essentially the same duties, with the addition of extensive follow-up maintenance. They would analyze business needs and suggest proper systems to answer them. In addition, more and more independent consulting firms are hiring systems programmer-analysts to perform the same tasks.

Analysts with advanced degrees in computer science or computer engineering will be in great demand. Individuals with master's degrees in business administration with emphasis in information systems will also be highly desirable.

FOR MORE INFORMATION

For more information about systems programmer-analyst positions, contact

Association of Information Technology Professionals
401 North Michigan Avenue, Suite 2400
Chicago, IL 60611-4267
Tel: 800-224-9371
http://www.aitp.org

For information on becoming an independent consultant, contact
Independent Computer Consultants Association
11131 South Towne Square, Suite F
St. Louis, MO 63123-7817
Tel: 800-774-4222
Email: info@icca.org
http://www.icca.org

For information on certification, contact
Institute for Certification of Computing Professionals
2350 East Devon Avenue, Suite 115
Des Plaines, IL 60018-4610
Tel: 800-843-8227
Email: office@iccp.org
http://www.iccp.org

Computer Trainers

OVERVIEW

Computer trainers teach topics related to all aspects of using computers in the workplace, including personal computer (PC) software, operating systems for both stand-alone and networked systems, management tools for networks, and software applications for mainframe computers and specific industry management. Trainers work for training companies and software developers, either on the permanent staff or as independent consultants. They may produce training materials, including disk-based multimedia technology-delivered learning, instructor-led courseware, skills assessment, videos, and classroom teaching manuals.

HISTORY

The field of computer training has been around since about 1983, when the computer industry exploded with the introduction of the first PCs. With all of the new software packages being released, individual information technology (IT) and information services (IS) departments could not possibly keep up with the amount of training their employees needed. Software vendor companies started sending their employees out to teach new purchasers how to use their products, and a new section of the computer industry was born.

In the beginning, computer training was conducted like any other training, in a classroom setting with an instructor. Although that type of training is still prevalent today, current training methods incorporate new technology. According to the American Society for Training and Development (ASTD), workplace educators are turning to technology to deliver their instructions. Developments in hardware, computer networking, multimedia software, and video conferencing have tremendous potential for multiple-site instruction and training closer to people's work sites.

Technological developments constantly change the process in which work is done. As a result, computer trainers must be up to date on the latest developments and improvements in computer systems and programs. The ASTD also notes that training departments are finding new ways to deliver computer training, by using support networks of internal and external training providers, including consultants, community colleges, and universities.

THE JOB

The field of computer training encompasses several different areas. *Software vendor trainers* work for developer companies. *Consultants* work for themselves as independent contractors, often specializing in certain computer languages, skills, or platforms. Some trainers work in the corporate training departments of companies that develop products other than computers and software. Others are teachers and professors.

"As a software trainer, my duties are to be prepared to teach various topics related to our software to a variety of clients on any given day," says Marcy Anderson, a software trainer for Cyborg Systems, a human-resource software developer. "I teach from a training manual and demonstrate the procedures on my computer that displays the information on a large screen for the entire class. The class is given assignments throughout the day that they complete on their PCs. I assist them one on one with their questions as the class continues. Cyborg has a training center with four classrooms. I conduct classes in the training center, or I travel to the client and hold classes on-site."

Consultant trainers are certified to teach several different products, applications, environments, and databases, usually with companies such as Microsoft, IBM, or Apple. Most have been in the computer industry for many years, previously working as software programmers, architects, project managers, or developers.

Whatever their affiliation, most computer trainers use several ways to disseminate learning technologies, including CD-ROM, CBT-Text, electronic performance support systems, the Internet, Intranets, multimedia presentations, and video conferencing.

Trainers are beginning to explore the field of online learning. In the article, "Our Turn-of-the-Century Trend Watch," Paul Clothier, senior instructor, Softwire Corporation, says, "Improved online

A computer trainer (standing) assists a student. *(Don Mason, Corbis)*

learning (OL) design and technologies will significantly impact the technical training profession over the next few years. At present, much of the technical training taking place is in the form of instructor-led training (ILT) in a classroom. There are many advantages to ILT, but there are also considerable disadvantages, such as time investment, travel, and expense. To get a group of your most valuable technical people off to a week of training is often a major expense and inconvenience. Organizations are crying out for a better alternative, and OL increasingly is seen as an option."

REQUIREMENTS

High School
If you are interested in a career in computer training, take as many computer and mathematics classes as possible in high school. These will provide the foundation for the rest of your computer education. Start learning about computer programs, such as Visual Basic, on your own. Speech, drama, or other performance courses will also help get you used to speaking in front of a crowd. "A little showmanship doesn't hurt in keeping the class interested," notes Marcy Anderson.

Postsecondary Training
While there is no universally accepted way to prepare for a job in computer training, a bachelor's degree is generally required by most

employers. The best major for this field is not set in stone, however. Some majors that share skills with training include computer science, business, and education. To teach some of the more complex systems, a graduate degree might be necessary.

"In my personal experience, I did not pursue an education degree to become a trainer," says Anderson. "I have a business degree and years of experience in the human resources field. For software training, though, knowledge of software and computers is essential. A degree in education would provide excellent skills for this type of position. Additionally, a business or liberal arts major might provide the presentation skills that are valuable. Certainly any presentation or public speaking certifications would be desirable."

Obtaining graduate and postgraduate degrees enhances potential marketability, as well as future salaries.

Certification or Licensing

As a trainer, you should be certified in the products (such as Microsoft C++, MFC, Visual Basic, and Access), developments (including Internet, HTML, Java Script), applications (MS Office, for example), environments (such as OS/2, Windows, client/server), and databases (including ADO, Access, ODBC, BD/2, and SQL) you want to instruct. Classes in each of the disciplines are available from the manufacturers, and you must pass an examination before receiving certification. Trainers employed by hardware and software developers might receive on-the-job instruction on the most current product releases. Certification is not mandatory (except for consultants), but will provide you with a competitive advantage. ITrain, the International Association of Information Technology Trainers awards the professional technical trainer designation to association members who complete a seminar, submit a 30-minute video of one of their training presentations, and pay an application fee. Additionally, applicants must provide 10 student references and post-class evaluations. The American Society for Training and Development offers the certified professional in learning and performance designation to applicants who pass an examination.

Technological advances come so rapidly in the computer field that continuous study is necessary to keep your skills up to date. Continuing education is usually offered by employers, hardware and software vendors, colleges and universities, or private training institutions. Additional training can also come from professional associations.

Other Requirements

"Trainers need to be patient and extroverted," says Anderson. "A sense of humor is essential, along with a high level of energy. People who are very introverted, even though they might be good with computers, should not do software training." As a trainer, you will have to be ready to teach any class in your repertoire at any time, so you have to be adaptable and flexible to handle that uncertainty.

EXPLORING

One way to begin exploring this field now is to talk to someone who is a computer trainer. Marcy Anderson also suggests getting involved in speech or drama clubs. "Any experiences a high school student can get in making presentations or performing in front of a group help to build the skills necessary to be successful in this career," she says.

Internships are always helpful ways of obtaining some experience in the field before graduation. Working in the training department of a large corporation or software vendor would provide invaluable experience and contacts.

Teach yourself the various software packages, and read as much as you can about the industry. To stay updated in this field, read publications such as *Computer* magazine (http://www.computer.org/computer). Although jobs in the computer industry are abundant, there is always competition for desirable positions.

EMPLOYERS

Computer trainers work for a variety of employers, from large, international companies to community colleges. Many work for hardware and software manufacturers or training departments in the bigger companies. Others are employed by training companies that disseminate training information and tools. Still other computer trainers work independently as consultants. The rest are employed by schools, adult continuing education programs, and government institutions. Some software companies and consultants operate training sites on the Internet. Since almost every type of company will need computer training at one point or another, these companies are located throughout the country and, indeed, throughout the world.

STARTING OUT

There are several ways to obtain a position as a computer trainer. Some people are hired right out of college by software companies. "There are many software companies that hire smart college grads to work with clients and implement their software," notes Marcy

Anderson. Others start out in technical positions with software companies and then move into training as their expertise in the product increases.

Job candidates for computer trainer positions might obtain their jobs from on-campus recruitment, classified want ads, posting their resumes on the Internet, or word of mouth. Many large cities hold technology job fairs that host hundreds of companies, all of which are interested in hiring.

ADVANCEMENT

Computer trainers can move upward into positions such as training specialists, senior training specialists, and training managers, depending on the size of the company.

EARNINGS

In general, computer trainers' salaries increase with the level of their education and the amount of their experience. According to a 2007 salary survey conducted by the Redmond Media Group, the average salary of the responding Microsoft Certified Trainers (MCTs) was $82,322. These figures do not include yearly bonuses, which may add several thousand dollars to a trainer's income. Additionally, these salaries are for MCTs, so not all computer trainers will have incomes in this range. For example, Salary.com reports that technical trainers earned salaries that ranged from less than $41,774 to $76,293 or more in 2007. In addition to education and experience, other factors influencing earnings are the size of the employer and, if the trainer is working independently, the number of clients he or she has during the year.

Most computer trainers employed by corporations receive medical and dental insurance, paid vacations, sick days, and retirement plans. Some companies also offer reimbursement for continuing education courses and training.

WORK ENVIRONMENT

Computer trainers normally work in offices in comfortable surroundings. They usually work 40 hours a week, which is the same as many other professional or office workers. However, travel to clients' sites can be required and might increase the number of hours worked per week. They spend most of their time in classrooms or training facilities. "The best part of the job is that it is interesting and fun," says Marcy Anderson. "It is nice to be an 'expert' and impart knowledge to others, even though it can be hard sometimes to feel up and energized to teach every day."

OUTLOOK

There will be a great need for computer trainers in the coming years as computer technology continues to develop. Information from the EQW National Employer Survey indicates that employers are using a variety of external training providers. As this outsourcing grows, an increase in the number of training providers is likely. Such independent providers as community and technical colleges, universities, profit-oriented learning and development centers, and private industry associations will all be discovering new business opportunities in outsourcing, according to the ASTD. "The short life cycles of technology products, compounded by the greater complexity of many job roles, are expected to heighten the demand for external information-technology education providers and other training providers," the ASTD notes.

FOR MORE INFORMATION

For information on certification and career resources, contact
American Society for Training and Development
1640 King Street, Box 1443
Alexandria, VA 22313-2043
Tel: 703-683-8100
http://www.astd.org

For information on online training, contact
Computer Strategies
7677 Oakport Street, Suite 105
Oakland, CA 94621-1933
Tel: 800-633-2248
Email: info@my-ecoach.com
http://www.compstrategies.com

For information on certification, contact
ITrain, International Association of Information Technology Trainers
PMB 616
6030-M Marshalee Drive
Elkridge, MD 21075-5987
Tel: 888-290-6200
http://itrain.org

Database Specialists

QUICK FACTS

School Subjects
Computer science
Mathematics

Personal Skills
Mechanical/manipulative
Technical/scientific

Work Environment
Primarily indoors
Primarily one location

Minimum Education Level
Bachelor's degree

Salary Range
$37,350 to $64,670 to
$103,010+

Certification or Licensing
Voluntary

Outlook
Much faster than the average

DOT
039

GOE
02.06.01

NOC
2172

O*NET-SOC
15-1061.00

OVERVIEW

Database specialists design, install, update, modify, maintain, and repair computer database systems to meet the needs of their employers. To do this work they need strong math skills, the ability to work with many variables at once, and a solid understanding of the organization's objectives. They consult with other management officials to discuss computer equipment purchases, determine requirements for various computer programs, and allocate access to the computer system to users. They might also direct training of personnel who use company databases regularly. Database specialists may also be called *database designers, database analysts, database managers,* or *database administrators* in some businesses; at other businesses, these designations represent separate jobs. All of these positions, however, fall under the umbrella category of database specialist. There are approximately 104,000 database specialists working in the United States.

HISTORY

During the 1950s, computers were big—they easily filled entire warehouses—and they were not considered practical for anything other than large government and research projects. However, by 1954, the introduction of semiconductors made computers smaller and more accessible to businesses. Within 30 years, computers had influenced nearly every aspect of life, such as work, entertainment, and even shopping. Today, computers are everywhere. Technology has continued to make computers smaller, more productive, and more efficient.

Technological advances have made database computing a subfield of tremendous growth and potential. Businesses and other organizations use databases to replace existing paper-based procedures but also create new uses for them every day. For example, catalog companies use databases to organize inventory and sales systems, which before they did by hand. These same companies are pushing technology further by investigating ways to use databases to customize promotional materials. Instead of sending the same catalog out to everyone, some companies are looking to send each customer a special edition filled with items he or she would be sure to like, based on past purchases and a personal profile.

Database specialists are crucial to database development. In fact, many companies who took an inexpensive route to database computing by constructing them haphazardly are now sorry they did not initially hire a specialist. Designing the database structure is important because it translates difficult, abstract relationships into concrete, logical structures. If the work is done well to begin with, the database will be better suited to handle changes in the future.

Most commercial computer systems make use of some kind of database. As computer speed and memory capacity continue to increase, databases will become increasingly complex and able to handle many new uses. Therefore, the individuals and businesses that specialize in inputting, organizing, and making available various types of information stand at the forefront of an ever-growing field.

THE JOB

So just what is a database and how is it used? It may be easiest to think of a database as being the computer version of the old-fashioned file cabinet that is filled with folders containing information. The database is the information, and the database specialist is the person who designs or adjusts programs that determine how the information is stored, how separate pieces of information relate and affect one another, and how the overall system should be organized. For example, a specialist may set up a retailer's customer database to have a separate "record" for each customer, in the same way that the retailer may have had a separate file folder in its file cabinet for each customer. In the retailer's sales database, each sale represented by an invoice will have a separate record. Each record contains many "fields" where specific pieces of information are entered. Examples of fields for a customer database might include customer number, customer name, address, city, state, ZIP code, phone, and contact person. Examples of fields in a sales database might include customer number, item purchased, quantity, price, date of purchase, and total.

With information organized in separate fields, the retailer can easily sort customer records or invoices, just like filing folders in a file cabinet. In this way, the retailer could print a list of all its customers in Iowa, for example, or total sales for the month of April.

In the same way that records within a database can be sorted, databases themselves can be related to each other. The customer database can be related to the sales database by the common field: customer number. In this way, a business could print out a list of all purchases by a specific customer, for example, or a list of customers who purchased a specific product.

Database specialists are responsible for the flow of computer information within an organization. They make major decisions concerning computer purchases, system designs, and personnel training. Their duties combine general management ability with a detailed knowledge of computer programming and systems analysis.

The specific responsibilities of a database specialist are determined by the size and type of employer. For example, a database specialist for a telephone company may develop a system for billing customers, while a database specialist for a large store may develop a system for keeping track of in-stock merchandise. To do this work accurately, database specialists need a thorough knowledge and understanding of the company's computer operations.

There are three main areas of the database specialist's work: planning what type of computer system a company needs; implementing and managing the system; and supervising computer room personnel.

To adequately plan a computer system, database specialists must have extensive knowledge of the latest computer technology and the specific needs of their company. They meet with high-ranking company officials and decide how to apply the available technology to the company's needs. Decisions include what type of hardware and software to order and how the data should be stored. Database specialists must be aware of the cost of the proposed computer system as well as the budget within which the company is operating. Long-term planning is also important. Specialists must ensure that the computer system can process not only the existing level of computer information received, but also the anticipated load and type of information the company could receive in the future. Such planning is vitally important since, even for small companies, computer systems can cost several hundred thousand dollars.

Implementing and managing a computer system entails a variety of technical and administrative tasks. Depending on the organization's needs, the specialist may modify a system already in place, develop a whole new system, or tailor a commercial system to meet these needs. To do this type of work, the database specialist must be familiar with accounting principles and mathematical formulas. Scheduling access to the computer is also a key responsibility. Sometimes, database specialists work with representatives from all of a company's departments to create a schedule. The specialist prioritizes needs and monitors usage so that each department can do its work. All computer usage must be documented and stored for future reference.

Safeguarding the computer operations is another important responsibility of database specialists. They must make plans in case a computer system fails or malfunctions so that the information stored in the computer is not lost. A duplication of computer files may be a part of this emergency planning. A backup system must also be employed so that the company can continue to process information. Database specialists must also safeguard a system so that only authorized personnel have access to certain information. Computerized information may be of vital importance to a company, and database specialists ensure that it does not fall into the wrong hands.

Database specialists may also be responsible for supervising the work of personnel in the computer department. They may need to train new computer personnel hires to use the company's database, and they may also need to train all computer personnel when an existing database is modified. At some organizations, specialists are also required to train all employees in the use of an upgraded or a new system. Therefore, specialists need the ability to translate technical concepts into everyday language.

Database specialists may be known by a number of different titles and have a variety of responsibilities, depending on the size and the needs of the organizations that employ them. According to an article in *Computerworld,* the title *database designer* indicates someone who works on database programming. These workers usually have a math or engineering background. The title *database administrator* indicates someone who primarily focuses on the performance of the database, making sure everything is running smoothly. They may also do routine jobs, such as adding new users to the system. The title *database analyst* indicates someone who primarily focuses on the business, its goals, products, and customers. They work on improving the database so that the organization can meet its goals. In large businesses or organizations, the many duties of the database specialist may be strictly divided among a number of specialists. In smaller organizations there may be only one database specialist, designer, manager, administrator, or analyst who is responsible for carrying out all the tasks mentioned above. No matter what their title is, however, all database specialists work with an operation that processes millions of bits of information at a huge cost. This work

Mean Annual Earnings by Specialty, 2006

Rail transportation	$100,670
Natural gas distribution	$86,920
Other financial investment activities	$82,790
Audio and video equipment manufacturing	$82,250
Semiconductor and other electronic component manufacturing	$78,320
Computer systems design and related services	$74,570
Insurance carriers	$70,770
Management of companies and enterprises	$68,520
Local government	$62,500
Colleges, universities, and professional schools	$58,720

Source: U.S. Department of Labor

demands accuracy and efficiency in decision-making and problem-solving abilities.

REQUIREMENTS

High School

While you are in high school, take as many math, science, and computer classes as you can. These courses will provide you with the basis to develop your logical thinking skills and understanding of computers. Take electronics or other technical courses that will teach you about schematic drawing, working with electricity, and, again, develop logical thinking. You will also benefit from taking accounting courses and English classes, as you will need strong written and verbal communication skills.

Postsecondary Training

A bachelor's degree in computer science, computer information systems, or another computer-related discipline is recommended as the minimum requirement for those wishing to work as database specialists. Some exceptions have been made for people without a degree but who have extensive experience in database administration. Taking this route to become a database specialist, however, is becoming increasingly rare. The employers of tomorrow will expect you to have at least a four-year degree. Courses in a bachelor's degree program usually include data processing, systems analysis methods, more detailed software and hardware concepts, management principles, and information systems planning. To advance in the field, you will probably need to complete further education. Many businesses today, especially larger companies, prefer database managers to have a master's degree in computer science or business administration. Some companies offer to help with or pay for their employees' advanced education, so you may want to consider this possibility when looking for an entry-level job.

Certification or Licensing

Some database specialists become certified for jobs in the computer field by passing an examination given by the Institute for Certification of Computing Professionals (ICCP). For further information, contact the ICCP at the address given at the end of this article. The ICCP, in cooperation with DAMA International, offers the certified data management professional designation to applicants who pass three examinations. In addition, specialists who want to keep their skills current may take training programs offered by database developers, such as Oracle. These training programs may also lead to certifications.

Other Requirements

Database specialists are strong logical and analytical thinkers. They excel at analyzing massive amounts of information and organizing it into a coherent structure composed of complicated relationships. They are also good at weighing the importance of each element of a system and deciding which ones can be omitted without diminishing the quality of the final project.

Specialists also need strong communication skills. This work requires contact with employees from a wide variety of jobs. Specialists must be able to ask clear, concise, and technical questions of people who are not necessarily familiar with how a database works.

As is true for all computer professionals, specialists should be motivated to keep up with technological advances and able to learn new things quickly. Those who are interested in working almost exclusively in one industry (for example, banking) should be willing to gain as much knowledge as possible about that specific field in addition to their computer training. With an understanding of both fields of knowledge, individuals are more easily able to apply computer technology to the specific needs of the company.

EXPLORING

There are a number of ways to explore your interest in this field while you are still in high school. "Start by reading books on the subject," says Scott Sciaretta, an internal database consultant for Choicepoint in Atlanta, Georgia. "There are hundreds of them at most bookstores."

You can also join your high school's computer club to work on computer projects and meet others interested in the field. Learn everything you can about computers by working with them regularly. Online sources can be particularly good for keeping up to date with new developments and learning from people who are actively involved in this work. Learn to use a commercial database program, either by teaching yourself or taking a class. The Association for Computing Machinery has a Special Interest Group on Management of Data (SIGMOD). The Resources page of SIGMOD's Web site (http://www.acm.org/sigmod) provides an index of public domain database software that you may want to check out.

You may also want to ask your school guidance counselor or a computer teacher to arrange for a database specialist to speak to your class at school or to arrange for a field trip to a company to see database specialists at work. Another option is to ask your school administrators about databases used by the school and try to interview any database specialists working in or for the school system. Similar attempts could be made with charities in your area that make use of computer databases for membership and client records as well as mailing lists.

Look for direct-experience opportunities, such as part-time work, summer internships, and even summer camps that specialize in computers. "Try to get a job as an intern in a database shop and learn by watching, mentoring, and grunt work," Sciaretta recommends. If you can't find such a position, you can still put your skills to work by offering to set up small databases, such as address books, recipe databases, or DVD libraries for friends or family members.

EMPLOYERS

Approximately 104,000 database administrators are employed in the United States today. Any business or organization that uses databases as a part of its operations hires database professionals. Database specialists work for investment companies, telecommunications firms, banks, insurance companies, publishing houses, hospitals, school systems, universities, and a host of other large and midsize businesses and nonprofit organizations. There are also many opportunities with federal, state, and city governments.

STARTING OUT

Most graduating college students work closely with their school's career services office to obtain information about job openings and interviews. Local and national employers often recruit college graduates on campus, making it much easier for students to talk with many diverse companies. Another good source of information is through summer internships, which are completed typically between junior and senior year. Many major companies in the computer field, such as Intel (http://www.intel.com/jobs/students) and Oracle (http://www.oracle.com/corporate/employment/college/opportunities/internships.html), have established undergraduate intern programs. This experience is valuable for two reasons. First, it gives students hands-on exposure to computer-related jobs. Second, it allows students to network with working computer professionals who may help them find full-time work after graduation. Interested individuals might also scan the classified ads or work with temporary agencies or headhunters to find entry-level and midlevel positions. Professional organizations, such as SIGMOD, and professional publications are other sources of information about job openings.

ADVANCEMENT

The job of database specialist is in itself a high-level position. Advancement will depend to some extent on the size of the business the specialist works for, with larger companies offering more opportunities for growth at the mid-level and senior levels of management. Scott Sciaretta explains his career path and advancement this way: "I got my first job in the field by internal promotion. Basically, I was doing some computer programming for my department on the side to automate a few of the menial tasks. My work got noticed, and I was given the job of running the company's computer department when the position opened. At my current level, the advancement opportunities are not easy. For me to advance I either need to expand my scope or work for a larger company, both of which are very feasible with hard work. However, salary advancements are easy and can be quite large. There are many opportunities for advancement from entry-level or junior positions."

Another factor influencing advancement is the interests of each individual. Generally, people fall into two categories: those who want to work on the business side and those who prefer to stay in a technical job. For individuals who want to get into the managerial side of the business, formal education in business administration is usually required, usually in the form of a master's degree in business administration. In upper-level management positions, specialists must work on cross-functional teams with professionals in finance, sales, personnel, purchasing, and operations. Superior database specialists at larger companies may also be promoted to executive positions.

Some database specialists prefer to stay on the technical side of the business. For them, the hands-on computer work is the best part of their job. Advancement for these workers will, again, involve further education in terms of learning about new database systems, gaining certification in a variety of database programs, or even moving into another technology area such as software design or networking.

As specialists acquire education and develop solid work experience, advancement will take the form of more responsibilities and higher wages. One way to achieve this is to move to a better-paying, more challenging database position at a larger company. Some successful database specialists become high-paid consultants or start their own businesses. Teaching, whether as a consultant or at a university or community college, is another option for individuals with high levels of experience.

EARNINGS

A fairly wide range of salaries exists for database specialists. Earnings vary with the size, type, and location of the organization as well as a person's experience, education, and job responsibilities. According to the U.S. Department of Labor, median annual earnings for database administrators were $64,670 in 2006. The lowest paid 10 percent earned less than $37,350, while the highest paid 10 percent earned more than $103,010. Robert Half International reported that starting salaries for database administrators ranged from $68,250 to $98,750 in 2007.

Benefits for database professionals depend on the employer; however, they usually include such items as health insurance, retirement or 401(k) plans, and paid vacation days.

WORK ENVIRONMENT

Database specialists work in modern offices, usually located next to the computer room. If they work as consultants, they may travel to client sites as little as once or twice per project or as often as every week. Most duties are performed at a computer at the individual's desk. Travel is occasionally required for conferences and visits to affiliated database locations. Travel requirements vary with employer, client, and level of position held. Database specialists may need to attend numerous meetings, especially during planning stages of a project. They work regular 40-hour weeks but may put in over-time as deadlines approach. During busy periods, the work can be quite stressful since accuracy is very important. Database special-ists must therefore be able to work well under pressure and respond quickly to last-minute changes. Emergencies may also require spe-cialists to work overtime or long hours without a break, sometimes through the night.

"I like what I do. It's kind of like playing," Scott Sciaretta says. "The hours are flexible. You get to work on and set up million-dollar systems. There also is a high degree of visibility from upper management. The downside is that I work lots of hours, including many weekends, and I have a never-ending list of work. The hardest part of the job is juggling the schedules and configurations for many projects at one time."

OUTLOOK

The use of computers and database systems in almost all business settings creates tremendous opportunities for well-qualified data-base personnel. Database specialists and computer support special-ists are predicted by the U.S. Department of Labor to be among the fastest growing occupations through 2014.

Employment opportunities for database specialists should be best in large urban areas because of the many businesses and organiza-tions located there that need employees to work with their databases. Since smaller communities are also rapidly developing significant job opportunities, skilled workers can pick from a wide range of jobs throughout the country. Those with the best education and the most experience in computer systems and personnel management will find the best job prospects.

"The field of Unix systems and databases is wide open," notes Scott Sciaretta. "There is and will be greater demand for good talent than the industry can supply. Most companies are moving to larger databases, and the need for Oracle and Microsoft SQL Server data-base administrators in particular is a bottomless pit."

FOR MORE INFORMATION

For information on career opportunities or student chapters, contact
Association of Information Technology Professionals
401 North Michigan Avenue, Suite 2400
Chicago, IL 60611-4267
Tel: 800-224-9371
http://www.aitp.org

For information on certification, contact
DAMA International
19239 North Dale Mabry Highway, #132
Lutz, FL 33548-5067
Tel: 813-448-7786
http://www.dama.org

For information on scholarships, student membership, and to read
Careers in Computer Science and Computer Engineering, *visit the*
IEEE's Web site:
IEEE Computer Society
1730 Massachusetts Avenue, NW
Washington, DC 20036-1992
Tel: 202-371-0101
Email: membership@computer.org
http://www.computer.org

For more information about certification, contact
Institute for Certification of Computing Professionals
2350 East Devon Avenue, Suite 115
Des Plaines, IL 60018-4610
Tel: 800-843-8227
Email: office@iccp.org
http://www.iccp.org

To read articles from the quarterly bulletin Data Engineering, *pro-*
duced by the IEEE Technical Committee on Data Engineering,
visit
Data Engineering
http://research.microsoft.com/db

For more information on the Association for Computing Machinery's
special interest group on management of data, visit its Web site:
Special Interest Group on Management of Data
http://www.acm.org/sigmod

Graphics Programmers

OVERVIEW

Graphics programmers design software that allows computers to generate graphic designs, charts, and illustrations for manufacturing, communications, entertainment, and engineering. They also develop computer applications that graphic designers use to create multimedia presentations, posters, logos, layouts for publication, and many other objects.

HISTORY

Developed from technology used during World War II, the first modern computer was used in 1951 to organize the population data compiled in the 1950 U.S. Census. At that time, computers were considered nothing more than electronic systems for storing and retrieving information. Because of their immense size and development costs, plus the difficulty of installing and programming them, it was thought that computers would only be useful for huge projects such as a nationwide census. But private companies were quick to explore ways to harness the power of the computer to gain an edge over their competitors. Today, computer technology has been adapted for use in practically every field and industry, from manufacturing to medicine, from telephones to space exploration, from engineering to entertainment.

Computers are used not only to store and organize data; they also communicate data to other computers and to users. Computer scientists have made great strides in adapting computer technology for visual presentation. Graphics are an important communications tool and are now used in many diverse industries to interpret and display

QUICK FACTS

School Subjects
Art
Computer science

Personal Skills
Artistic
Technical/scientific

Work Environment
Primarily indoors
Primarily one location

Minimum Education Level
Bachelor's degree

Salary Range
$38,460 to $65,510 to $106,610+

Certification or Licensing
Voluntary

Outlook
More slowly than the average

DOT
030

GOE
01.04.02

NOC
2163

O*NET-SOC
15-1021.00

the relationships between various data elements. They can be used to illustrate difficult or abstract concepts, show ratios and proportions, or demonstrate how forces such as the weather change over time. As the graphics field has expanded, the emphasis has shifted from two-dimensional solutions, such as brochures or posters, to three-dimensional design, including screen displays for television and Web pages. Computer graphics can also be used for interactive automobile design, medical simulations, animation, flight simulations, digital movie special effects, and virtual reality.

Although "hand skills," such as drawing and drafting are still used in graphics design, the computer has become the primary tool. The advantages of using computers are many, including speed, precision, and on-screen editing.

THE JOB

The graphics programmer's job is similar to that of other computer programmers: determining what the computer will be expected to do and writing instructions for the computer that will allow it to carry out these functions. For a computer to perform any operation at all, detailed instructions must be written into its memory in a computer language, such as BASIC, COBOL, Pascal, C++, HTML, Smalltalk, and Java. The programmer is responsible for telling the computer exactly what to do.

A graphics programmer's job can be illustrated by tracing how a program designed for desktop publishing is developed. Working with a computer systems analyst, the graphics programmer's first step is to interview managers or clients to determine the kinds of tasks the program will be expected to perform, such as drawing shapes, organizing text, and adding different colors. The programmer investigates current computer graphics capabilities and how to improve them.

Once the expectations of the program are identified, the programmer usually prepares a flowchart, which illustrates on paper how the computer will process the incoming information and carry out its operations. The programmer then begins to write the instructions for the computer in a programming language, such as FORTRAN or C. The coded instructions will also contain comments so other programmers can understand it.

Once the program is written, it is tested thoroughly by programmers, graphic designers, and quality assurance testers to make sure it can do the desired tasks. If problems, or glitches, do exist, the program must be altered and retested until it produces correct results. This is known as debugging the program.

Once the program is ready to be put into operation, the programmer prepares the written instructions for the people who will be operating and consulting the graphics program in their daily work.

Many diverse industries use computer graphics. In medicine, for example, physicians, nurses, and technicians can use computer graphics to view the internal organs of patients. Scanners feed vital information about a patient's body to a computer that interprets the input and displays a graphic representation of the patient's internal conditions. Computer graphics are used in flight simulators by airlines and NASA to train pilots and astronauts. Weather forecasters and television newscasters use graphics to explain statistical information, such as weather or stock market reports. Business people use computer-generated graphs and charts to make their reports more interesting and informative. Engineers use computer graphics to test the wear and stress of building materials and machine parts. The movie industry has found ingenious ways to use computer graphics for special effects. Professional artists have explored computer graphics for creating works of art.

Graphics programmers can be employed either by software manufacturing companies or by the companies that buy and use the software (known as the end user). The programmer who works for a software manufacturer will work on programs designed to fit the needs of prospective customers. For example, the programmer might work on a report-writing program for businesses, and so develop simple ways for people to display and print statistical data in the form of diagrams, pie charts, and bar graphs. Programmers, working alone or as part of a team, must make the product user friendly.

Computer graphics programmers who work for end users have to tailor commercial software to fit their company's individual needs. If a company has limited computer needs or cannot afford to keep a programmer on payroll, it can call an independent consulting firm that has graphics programmers on staff and hire consultants for specific projects.

REQUIREMENTS
High School
If you are interested in computer graphics programming, take classes that satisfy the admission requirements of the college or university that you plan to attend. Most major universities have requirements for English, mathematics, science, and foreign languages. Other classes that are useful include physics, statistics, logic, computer science, and if available, drafting. Since graphics programmers have

to have an artistic sense of layout and design, art and photography courses can also be helpful.

Postsecondary Training

A bachelor's degree in computer science or a related field is essential for anyone wishing to enter the field of computer graphics programming. It is not a good idea, however, to major in graphics programming exclusively, unless you plan to go on to earn a master's degree or doctorate in the field. According to the Special Interest Group on Computer Graphics, a division of the Association for Computing Machinery (ACM SIGGRAPH), it is better for you to concentrate on the area in which you plan to use computer graphics skills, such as art or engineering, rather than focusing on graphics classes.

Others complete a general computer science curriculum, choosing electives such as graphics or business programming if they are available. Because there are many specialties within the field of computer graphics, such as art, mapmaking, animation, and computer-aided design (CAD), you should examine the courses of study offered in several schools before choosing the one you wish to attend. An associate's degree or a certificate from a technical school may enable you to get a job as a keyboard operator or other paraprofessional with some firms, but future advancement is unlikely without additional education. Competition for all types of programming jobs is increasing and will limit the opportunities of those people with less than a bachelor's degree.

Certification or Licensing

No specific certification is available for graphics programmers. Two general computer-related certifications (certified computing professional and the associate computing professional) are available from the Institute for Certification of Computing Professionals, whose address is listed at the end of this article. Although it is not required, certification may boost your attractiveness to employers during the job search.

Other Requirements

Successful graphics programmers need a high degree of reasoning ability, patience, and persistence, as well as an aptitude for mathematics. You should also have strong writing and speaking skills, so that you can communicate effectively with your coworkers and supervisors.

EXPLORING

If you are interested in a career in computer graphics programming, you might want to check out *Computer Graphics Quarterly,* a publication of the Special Interest Group on Computer Graphics. You can

read back issues of this interesting publication online at http://www
.siggraph.org/publications/newsletter.

You might also contact the computer science department of a
local university to get more information about the field. It may be
possible to speak with a faculty member whose specialty is computer
graphics or to sit in on a computer graphics class. Find out if there
are any computer manufacturers or software firms in your area. By
contacting their public relations departments, you might be able to
speak with someone who works with or designs computer graphics
systems and learn how one works.

If you are interested in the artistic applications of graphics, get
involved with artistic projects at school, like theater set design,
poster and banner design for extracurricular activities, or yearbook
or literary magazine design.

EMPLOYERS

Graphics programmers are employed throughout the United States.
Opportunities are best in large cities and suburbs where business
and industry are active. Programmers who develop software systems
work for software manufacturers, many of which are in central California. There is also a concentration of software manufacturers in
Boston, Chicago, and Atlanta. Programmers who adapt and tailor
the software to meet specific needs of clients are employed around
the country by the end users.

Graphics programmers can also work in service centers that fur-
nish computer time and software to businesses. Agencies, called job
shops, employ programmers on short-term contracts. Self-employed
graphics programmers can also work as consultants to small companies that cannot afford to employ full-time programmers.

STARTING OUT

Counselors and professors should be able to keep you informed of
companies hiring computer programmers, including graphics programmers. Large manufacturing companies and computer software
firms who employ many computer programmers send recruiters to
universities with computer science departments, usually working
cooperatively with the guidance and placement departments. Guidance departments can also tell you about any firms offering work-
study programs and internships, which are excellent ways to gain
training and experience in graphics programming. As employers
become increasingly selective about new hires and seek to hold down
the costs of in-house training, internships in computer programming
are a great opportunity not only for on-the-job experience but also
for a possible position after graduation from college.

Other possible sources of entry-level jobs are the numerous placement agencies that specialize in the field of computers. These agencies often advertise in major newspapers, technical journals, and computer magazines. They can also help match programmers to temporary jobs as more firms lower their personnel costs and hire freelance programmers to meet their needs. Programmers can also find out about new job opportunities by attending computer graphics conferences and networking with their professional peers. Some job openings are advertised in newspapers or online.

ADVANCEMENT

The computer industry experiences high turnover, as large numbers of programmers and other employees change companies and/or specialties. Some programmers leave their positions to accept higher-paying jobs with other firms, while others leave to start their own consulting companies. These extremely mobile conditions offer many opportunities both for job seekers and for those looking for career advancement.

In most companies, especially larger firms, advancement depends on an employee's experience and length of service. Beginning programmers might work alone on simple assignments after some initial instruction or on a team with more experienced programmers. Either way, beginning programmers generally must work under close supervision.

Because technology changes so rapidly, programmers must continuously update their training by taking courses sponsored by their employers or software vendors. For skilled workers who keep up to date with the latest technology, the prospects for advancement are good. In large organizations, they can be promoted to lead programmer and given supervisory responsibilities. Graphics programmers might be promoted to programmer-analysts, systems analysts, or to managerial positions. As employers increasingly contract out programming jobs, more opportunities should arise for experienced programmers with expertise in specific areas to work as consultants.

EARNINGS

According to the National Association of Colleges and Employers, starting salary offers for graduates with a bachelor's degree in computer science were $51,070 in 2007. The U.S. Department of Labor reports that median annual earnings of computer programmers were $65,510 in 2006. The lowest paid 10 percent earned less than $38,460; the highest 10 percent earned more than $106,610.

Programmers who work as independent consultants earn high salaries, but their salary may not be regular. Overall, those who work for private industry earn the most. Industry offers graphics programmers the highest earnings, as opportunities have expanded in aerospace, electronics, electrical machinery, and public utilities. Most of the best opportunities in this field are found in the Silicon Valley in northern California or in Seattle, Washington, where Microsoft has its headquarters.

Those who work for corporations or computer firms usually receive full benefits, such as health insurance, paid vacation, and sick leave.

WORK ENVIRONMENT

Most programmers work with state-of-the-art equipment. They usually put in eight to 12 hours a day and work a 40- to 50-hour week. To meet deadlines or finish rush projects, they may work evenings and weekends. Programmers work alone or as part of a team and often consult with the end users of the graphics program, as well as engineers and other specialists.

Programmers sometimes travel to attend seminars, conferences, and trade shows. Graphics programmers who work for software manufacturers may need to travel to assist current clients in their work or to solicit new customers for the software by demonstrating and discussing the product with potential buyers.

Graphics programmers in visual illustration departments of film or television production may spend months designing graphics for a clip that lasts minutes. There is often considerable pressure due to these deadlines.

OUTLOOK

According to the U.S. Department of Labor, the demand for computer specialists should be strong for the next decade, but employment for programmers will grow more slowly than for other computer science professionals. Technological developments have made it easier to write basic code, eliminating some of the need for programmers to do this work. More sophisticated software has allowed more and more end users to design, write, and implement more of their own programs. As a result, many of the programming functions are transferred to other types of workers. In addition, programmers will continue to face increasing competition from international programming businesses where work can be contracted out at a lower cost.

However, the specialty of graphics programming should still have a promising future. As more applications for computer graphics are explored and businesses find ways to use graphics in their everyday operations, graphics programmers will be in demand.

FOR MORE INFORMATION

For timelines, photos, and the history of computer developments, visit or contact
Computer History Museum
1401 North Shoreline Boulevard
Mountain View, CA 94043-1311
Tel: 650-810-1010
Email: info@computerhistory.org
http://www.computerhistory.org

For information on certification, contact
Institute for Certification of Computing Professionals
2350 East Devon Avenue, Suite 115
Des Plaines, IL 60018-4610
Tel: 800-843-8227
Email: office@iccp.org
http://www.iccp.org

For information on scholarships, student membership, and to read Careers in Computer Science and Computer Engineering, *visit the IEEE's Web site*
IEEE Computer Society
1730 Massachusetts Avenue, NW
Washington, DC 20036-1992
Tel: 202-371-0101
Email: membership@computer.org
http://www.computer.org

For information on membership, conferences, and publications, contact ACM SIGGRAPH:
Special Interest Group on Computer Graphics (SIGGRAPH)
Association for Computing Machinery
1515 Broadway, 17th Floor
New York, NY 10036-8901
Tel: 800-342-6626
http://www.siggraph.org

For a historical timeline of computer graphics and animation, visit
CGI Historical Timeline
http://accad.osu.edu/~waynec/history/timeline.html

For information about careers in information technology, visit
CyberCareers.org
http://www.cybercareers.org

Hardware Engineers

OVERVIEW

Computer *hardware engineers* design, build, and test computer hardware (such as computer chips and circuit boards) and computer systems. They also work with peripheral devices such as printers, scanners, modems, and monitors, among others. Hardware engineers are employed by a variety of companies, some of which specialize in business, accounting, science, or engineering. Most hardware engineers have a degree in computer science or engineering or equivalent computer background. There are approximately 77,000 computer hardware engineers employed in the United States.

HISTORY

What started as a specialty of electrical engineering has developed into a career field of its own. Today, many individuals interested in a career in one of the computer industry's most promising sectors turn to computer engineering. Computer engineers improve, repair, and implement changes needed to keep up with the demand for faster and stronger computers and complex software programs. Some specialize in the design of the hardware: computer or peripheral parts such as memory chips, motherboards, or microprocessors. Others specialize in creating and organizing information systems for businesses and the government.

More and more businesses rely on computers for information networking, accessing the Internet, and data processing for their daily activities. Also, computers are now affordable, allowing many families to purchase systems. Peripherals, such as printers, scanners, and disk drives, are popular accessories available to complete a variety of tasks. Computer engineers are also needed to develop

QUICK FACTS

School Subjects
Computer science
Mathematics

Personal Skills
Mechanical/manipulative
Technical/scientific

Work Environment
Primarily indoors
Primarily one location

Minimum Education Level
Bachelor's degree

Salary Range
$53,910 to $88,470 to
$135,260+

Certification or Licensing
Voluntary

Outlook
About as fast as the average

DOT
030

GOE
02.07.01

NOC
2147

O*NET-SOC
17-2061.00

A hardware engineer works in his laboratory. *(Dave Umberger, AP Images)*

and improve technology needed for consumer products, such as cellular phones, microwave ovens, compact disc players, digital video disc players, high-definition televisions, and video games. Engineers turn to program tools, such as computer-aided design (CAD), to help them create new products. CAD programs are often used with computer-aided manufacturing (CAM) programs to produce three-dimensional drawings that can easily be altered or manipulated, and direct the actual production of hardware components.

THE JOB

Computer hardware engineers work with the physical parts of computers, such as CPUs (computer processing units), motherboards, chipsets, video cards, cooling units, magnetic tape, disk drives, storage devices, network cards, and all the components that connect them, down to wires, nuts, and bolts.

Hardware engineers design parts and create prototypes to test, using CAD/CAM technology to make schematic drawings. They assemble the parts using fine hand tools, soldering irons, and microscopes. Parts are reworked and developed through multiple testing procedures. Once a final design is completed, hardware engineers oversee the manufacture and installation of parts.

Computer hardware engineers also work on peripherals, such as keyboards, printers, monitors, mice, track balls, modems, scanners, external storage devices, speaker systems, and digital cameras.

Some hardware engineers are involved in maintenance and repair of computers, networks, and peripherals. They troubleshoot problems, order or make new parts, and install them. Calvin Prior is a network systems administrator for TASC, a nonprofit social service agency headquartered in Chicago, Illinois. He is responsible for the day-to-day operations of a state-wide network of more than 300 servers. Prior starts work early; most mornings he's at his desk by 7:30 A.M. His first task of the day is making sure the network files from the previous day backed up successfully. Then he checks for email and voice mail messages and promptly responds to urgent problems.

Daily meetings are held to keep informed on department business. "It's very short and informal," says Prior. "We discuss urgent business or upcoming projects and schedules." The rest of the morning is spent working on various projects, troubleshooting systems, or phone work with TASC's remote offices. After a quick lunch break and if no network breakdowns or glitches occur, Prior usually spends his afternoons researching hardware products or responding to user requests. Since computer technology changes so rapidly, it is important to keep up with the development of new parts and the procedures for incorporating them into older systems as soon as they become available.

The workload changes daily, leaving some days more hectic than others. "It's important to be flexible," says Prior. "And be good at multi-tasking." If a major problem cannot be solved over the phone, Prior must travel to the source. Solutions are not always simple; some require changing hardware or redesigning the system. Prior often upgrades or reworks systems in the early morning, late at night, or on weekends to minimize the disruption of work. Major network problems require a complete shutdown of the entire system. "The fewer servers on the network, the better," he says.

Engineering professionals like Prior must be familiar with different network systems such as local area networks (LAN), wide area networks (WAN), among others, as well as programming languages suited to their company's needs. Many work as part of a team of specialists who use elements of science, math, and electronics to improve existing technology or implement solutions.

REQUIREMENTS

High School

Calvin Prior credits high school computer and electronics classes and programming courses for giving him a good head start in this career. You should also take math and physics, as well as speech and writing courses so that you will be able to communicate effectively with coworkers and clients.

Postsecondary Training

Hardware engineers need at least a bachelor's degree in computer engineering or electrical engineering. Employment in research laboratories or academic institutions might require a master's or Ph.D. in computer science or engineering. For a list of accredited four-year computer engineering programs, contact the Accreditation Board for Engineering and Technology.

College studies might include such computer science courses as computer architecture, systems design, chip design, microprocessor design, and network architecture, in addition to a heavy concentration of math and science classes.

Certification or Licensing

Not all computer professionals are certified. The deciding factor seems to be if it is required by their employer. Many companies offer tuition reimbursement, or incentives, to those who earn certification. Certification is available in a variety of specialties. The Institute for Certification of Computing Professionals (ICCP), offers the associate computing professional (ACP) designation for those new to the field and the certified computing professional (CCP) designation for those with at least 48 months of full-time professional-level work in computer-based information systems. Certification is considered by many to be a measure of industry knowledge as well as leverage when negotiating salary.

Other Requirements

Hardware engineers need a broad knowledge of and experience with computer systems and technologies. You need strong problem-solving and analysis skills and good interpersonal skills. Patience, self-motivation, and flexibility are important. Often, a number of projects are worked on simultaneously, so the ability to multitask is important. Because of rapid technological advances in the computer field, continuing education is a necessity.

EMPLOYERS

Approximately 77,000 computer hardware engineers are employed in the United States. Computer hardware engineers are employed in nearly every industry by small and large corporations alike. According to the *Occupational Outlook Quarterly*, approximately 43 percent of hardware engineers are employed in computer and electronic product manufacturing.

Jobs are available nationwide, though salary averages, as reported by a recent *Computerworld* survey, tend to be higher in New York City and Los Angeles. Note, however, that these cities are notorious for their high cost of living, which, in the end, may offset a higher income.

STARTING OUT

Education and solid work experience will open industry doors. Though a bachelor's degree is a minimum requirement for most corporate giants, some companies, smaller ones especially, will hire based largely on work experience and practical training. Many computer professionals employed in the computer industry for some time do not have traditional electrical engineering or computer science degrees, but rather moved up on the basis of their work record. However, if you aspire to a management position, or want to work as a teacher, then a college degree is a necessity.

Large computer companies aggressively recruit on campus armed with signing bonuses and other incentives. Employment opportunities are posted in newspaper want ads daily, with some papers devoting a separate section to computer-related positions. The Internet offers a wealth of employment information plus several sites for browsing job openings, or to post your resume. Most companies maintain a Web page where they post employment opportunities or solicit resumes.

ADVANCEMENT

Many companies hire new grads to work as junior engineers. Problem-solving skills and the ability to implement solutions is a big part of this entry-level job. With enough work experience, junior engineers can move into positions that focus on a particular area in the computer industry, such as networks or peripherals. Landing a senior-level engineering position, such as systems architect, for example, is possible after considerable work experience and study. Aspiring hardware engineers should hone their computer skills to the highest level through continuing education, certification, or even advanced graduate study. Many high-level engineers hold a master's degree or better.

Some computer professionals working on the technical side of the industry opt to switch over to the marketing side of the business. Advancement opportunities here may include positions in product management or sales.

EARNINGS

Starting salary offers in 2005 for bachelor's degree candidates in computer engineering averaged $52,464, according to a National Association of Colleges and Employers. Master's degree candidates averaged $60,354.

The U.S. Department of Labor reports that median annual earnings of computer hardware engineers were $88,470 in 2006. Salaries ranged from less than $53,910 to more than $135,260. Job perks, besides the usual benefit package of insurance, vacation, sick time, and profit sharing, may include stock options, continuing education or training, tuition reimbursement, flexible hours, and child care or other on-site services.

WORK ENVIRONMENT

Most hardware engineers work 40- to 50-hour weeks or more depending on the project to which they are assigned. Weekend work is common with some positions. Contrary to popular perceptions, hardware engineers do not spend their workdays cooped up in their offices. Instead, they spend the majority of their time meeting, planning, and working with various staff members from different levels of management and technical expertise. Since it takes numerous workers to take a project from start to finish, team players are in high demand.

OUTLOOK

Employment for hardware engineers will grow about as fast as the average for all occupations through 2014, according to the U.S. Department of Labor. Foreign competition and increased productivity at U.S. companies will limit opportunities for hardware engineers. Despite this prediction, opportunities are still expected to be good as the number of new graduates entering the field will match the number of engineers leaving the field.

FOR MORE INFORMATION

For a list of accredited programs in computer engineering, contact
Accreditation Board for Engineering and Technology
111 Market Place, Suite 1050
Baltimore, MD 21202-4012
Tel: 410-347-7700
http://www.abet.org

For information regarding the computer industry, career opportunities as a computer engineer, or the association's membership requirements, contact
Association for Computing Machinery
1515 Broadway
New York, NY 10036-8901

Tel: 800-342-6626
Email: acmhelp@acm.org
http://www.acm.org

For information on career opportunities for women in computing, contact
Association for Women in Computing
41 Sutter Street, Suite 1006
San Francisco, CA 94104-5414
Tel: 415-905-4663
Email: info@awc-hq.org
http://www.awc-hq.org

For information on a career in computer engineering and computer scholarships, contact
IEEE Computer Society
1730 Massachusetts Avenue, NW
Washington, DC 20036-1992
Tel: 202-371-0101
http://www.computer.org

For information on certification, contact
Institute for Certification of Computing Professionals
2350 East Devon Avenue, Suite 115
Des Plaines, IL 60018-4610
Tel: 800-843-8227
Email: office@iccp.org
http://www.iccp.org

For employment information, links to online career sites for computer professionals, information on membership for college students, and background on the industry, contact
Institute of Electrical and Electronics Engineers
3 Park Avenue, 17th Floor
New York, NY 10016-5997
Tel: 212-419-7900
Email: member-services@ieee.org
http://www.ieee.org

For comprehensive information about careers in electrical engineering and computer science, visit
Sloan Career Cornerstone Center
http://careercornerstone.org

Internet Developers

QUICK FACTS

School Subjects
Computer science
Mathematics

Personal Skills
Communication/ideas
Technical/scientific

Work Environment
Primarily indoors
Primarily one location

Minimum Education Level
Bachelor's degree

Salary Range
$30,000 to $62,532 to
$80,000

Certification or Licensing
Voluntary

Outlook
Faster than the average

DOT
N/A

GOE
N/A

NOC
2175

O*NET-SOC
15-1099.04

OVERVIEW

An *Internet developer,* otherwise known as a *Web developer* or *Web designer,* is responsible for the creation of an Internet site. Most of the time, this is a public Web site, but it can also be a private Internet network. Web developers are employed by a wide range of employers from small entrepreneurs to large corporate businesses to Internet consulting firms.

HISTORY

With the explosive growth of the World Wide Web, companies have flocked to use Internet technology to communicate worldwide—with employees, customers, clients, buyers, future stockholders, and so on. As a result, these companies need people who can create sites to fit their needs and the needs of their target audience.

In the early years of the Internet, most information presented was text only with no pictures. Today, a few sites still use a text-only format, but the vast majority have evolved to use the latest technologies, using graphics, video, audio, and interactive forms and applications.

For most companies, the first Internet sites were created and maintained by a sole individual who was a jack-of-all-trades. Today, these sites are often designed, implemented, and managed by entire departments composed of numerous individuals who specialize in specific areas of Web site work. The Web developer is the individual with the technical knowledge of programming to implement the ideas and goals of the organization into a smoothly flowing, informative, interesting Web site. Because of evolving technology, Web developers will require more specialized skills and technological expertise in the future.

THE JOB

After determining the overall goals, layout, and performance limitations of a client's Web site with input from marketing, sales, advertising, and other departments, an Internet or Web developer designs the site and writes the code necessary to run and navigate it. To make the site, working knowledge of the latest Internet programming languages such as Perl, Visual Basic, Java, C++, HTML, and XML is a must. The developer must also be up to date on the latest in graphic file formats and other Web production tools.

The concept of the site must be translated to a general layout. The layout must be turned into a set of pages, which are designed, written, and edited. Those pages are then converted into the proper code so that they can be placed on the server. There are software packages that exist to help the developer create the sites. However, software packages often use templates to create sites that have the same general look to them—which is not a good thing if the site is to stand out and look original. Also, no one software package does it all. Additional scripts or special features, such as banners with the latest advertising slogans, spinning logos, forms that provide data input from users, and easy online ordering, are often needed to add punch to a site.

Perhaps the trickiest part of the job is effectively integrating the needs of the organization with the needs of the customer. For example, the organization might want the content to be visually cutting-edge and entertaining, however, the targeted customer might not have the Internet connection speed needed to view those highly graphical pages and might prefer to get "just the facts" quickly. The developer must find a happy medium and deliver the information in a practical yet interesting manner.

REQUIREMENTS

High School

In high school, take as many courses as possible in computer science, science, and mathematics. These classes will provide you with a good foundation in computer basics and analytical-thinking skills. You should also take English and speech classes in order to hone your written and verbal communication skills.

Postsecondary Training

There currently is no established educational track for Internet developers. They typically hold bachelor's degrees in computer science or computer programming—although some have degrees in noncomputer areas, such as marketing, graphic design, library and information science, or information systems. Regardless of educational background, you need to have an understanding of computers and computer networks and a knowledge of Internet programming languages. Formal college training in these languages may be hard to come by because of the rapid evolution of the Internet. What's hot today might be obsolete tomorrow. Because of this volatility, most of the postsecondary training comes from hands-on experience. This is best achieved through internships or entry-level positions. One year of experience working on a site is invaluable toward landing a job in the field.

Certification or Licensing
Because there is no central governing organization or association for this field, certification is not required. Certifications are available, however, from various vendors of development software applications. These designations are helpful in proving your abilities to an employer. The more certifications you have, the more you have to offer. The Institute for Certification of Computing Professionals also offers certification.

Other Requirements
A good Internet developer balances technological know-how with creativity. You must be able to make a site stand out from the sea of other sites on the Web. For example, if your company is selling a product on the Web, your site needs to "scream" the unique qualities and benefits of the product.

Working with Internet technologies, you must be able to adapt quickly to change. It is not uncommon to learn a new programming language and get comfortable using it, only to have to learn another new language and scrap the old one. If you're a quick study, you should have an advantage.

EXPLORING
There are many ways to learn more about this career. You can read national news magazines, newspapers, and trade magazines or surf the Web for information about Internet careers. You can also visit a variety of Web sites to study what makes them either interesting or not so appealing. Does your high school have a Web site? If so, get involved in the planning and creation of new content for it. If not, talk to your computer teachers about creating one, or create your own site at home.

EMPLOYERS
Everyone is getting online these days, from the Fortune 500 companies to the smallest of mom-and-pop shops. The smaller companies

Books to Read

VGM Books. *Resumes for Computer Careers.* 3d ed. New York: McGraw-Hill, 2008.

Allen, Huey, and Joanne C. Wachter. *Careers in the Computer Field (Success Without College Series).* Hauppauge, N.J.: Barron's Educational Series, 2000.

Burns, Julie Kling. *Opportunities in Computer Careers.* New York: McGraw-Hill, 2001.

Farr, Michael. *Top 100 Computer and Technical Careers: Your Complete Guidebook to Major Jobs in Many Fields at All Training Levels.* 3d ed. Indianapolis, Ind.: JIST Works, 2006.

Gardner, Garth. *Careers in Computer Graphics & Animation.* Washington, D.C.: Garth Gardner Company, 2001.

Pasternak, Ceel, and Linda Thornburg. *Cool Careers for Girls in Computers.* Manassas Park, Va.: Impact Publications, 1999.

Stair, Lila B., and Leslie Stair. *Careers in Computers.* 3d ed. New York: McGraw-Hill, 2002.

Thornburg, Linda. *Cool Careers for Girls in Cybersecurity and National Safety.* Manassas Park, Va.: Impact Publications, 2004.

might have one person in charge of everything Web related: the server, the site, the security, and so on. Larger companies employ a department of many workers, each one taking on specific responsibilities.

An obvious place of employment is Internet consulting firms. Some firms specialize in Web development or Web site management; other firms offer services relating to all aspects of Web site design, creation, management, and maintenance.

The Internet is worldwide; thus, Internet jobs are available worldwide. Wherever there is a business connected to the Internet, people with the right skills can find Web-related jobs.

STARTING OUT

If you are looking for a job as an Internet developer, remember that experience is key. College courses are important, but if you graduate and have lots of book knowledge and no experience, you're going to get a slow start. If at all possible, seek out internships while in school.

Use the Internet to find a job. The search engines of popular Web sites aimed at job seekers (Yahoo! Hot Jobs, http://hotjobs.yahoo.com; Monster, http://www.monster.com; and CareerBuilder.com, http://www.careerbuilder.com) can be useful. While you're online, check out some of the Internet trade magazines for a job bank or classifieds section.

ADVANCEMENT

The next step up the career ladder for Internet developers might be a move to a larger company where the Web site presence consists of more pages. Some Web sites have hundreds and even thousands of pages! Another option is to become a *Webmaster*. Webmasters generally have the responsibility of overseeing all aspects (technical, management, maintenance, marketing, and organization) of a Web site.

EARNINGS

An entry-level position in Web development at a small company pays around $30,000. According to *Computerworld*'s 2006 Salary Survey, Web developers had average salaries (including bonuses) of $62,532 in 2006. Web developers who have considerable expertise can earn salaries of more than $80,000 annually.

Differences in pay tend to follow the differences found in other careers: the Pacific, Middle-Atlantic, and New England regions of the United States pay more than the North Central, South Atlantic, and South Central regions, and men are generally paid more than women (although this may change as the number of women rivals the number of men employed in these jobs).

Benefits include paid vacation, holidays, sick days, health insurance, dental insurance, life insurance, personal days, and bonuses.

WORK ENVIRONMENT

Web developers work at computers in comfortable offices. Most of their work is done alone; however, developers consult frequently with the Webmaster and others who work to write or edit the content of a site.

OUTLOOK

The career of Internet developer, like the Internet itself, is growing at a faster than average rate. As more and more companies look to expand their business worldwide, they need technically skilled employees to create the sites to bring their products, services, and corporate images to the Internet. In a survey of information architects by the Argus Center for Information Architecture, respondents predicted that certification and graduate degrees will become increasingly important in this career. Postsecondary training in Internet technology is growing, including graduate degrees in information design, informatics, interactive arts, human-computer interaction, and communication design. Universities that now offer strong programs in computer science, writing, and design will be developing liberal arts programs in information architecture. Jobs will be plentiful in the next decade for anyone with this specialized training.

FOR MORE INFORMATION

For information on careers, education, and student memberships, contact

IEEE Computer Society
1730 Massachusetts Avenue, NW
Washington, DC 20036-1992
Tel: 202-371-0101
Email: membership@computer.org
http://www.computer.org

For certification information, contact

Institute for Certification of Computing Professionals
2350 East Devon Avenue, Suite 115
Des Plaines, IL 60018-4610
Tel: 800-843-8227
http://www.iccp.org

Internet Security Specialists

OVERVIEW

An *Internet security specialist* is responsible for protecting a company's network, which can be accessed through the Internet, from intrusion by outsiders. These intruders are referred to as *hackers* (or *crackers*), and the process of breaking into a system is called *hacking* (or *cracking*). Internet security often falls under the jurisdiction of computer systems engineering and network administration within a company. Any company that has an Internet presence might employ an Internet security specialist. This includes all kinds of companies of all sizes anywhere around the world. Other Internet security specialists work for consulting firms that specialize in Internet security. Internet security specialists are sometimes known as *Internet security administrators, Internet security engineers, information security technicians,* and *network security consultants.*

HISTORY

Hacking first began in the telecommunications industry. Cracking a telephone system was called *phreaking* and involved learning how the telephone system worked and then manipulating it. As PCs began to hook up to networks via telephone lines and modems, phreaking took on new meaning and the information at risk took on greater importance.

November 2, 1988, is sometimes called Black Thursday by pioneers of the Internet community. On that day, a single program, later called a worm, was released onto the early form of the Internet (then called the ARPANET) and quickly rendered thousands of connected computers useless. The creator of the program, Robert Morris Jr., shocked at how quickly it was spreading, sent an anonymous message to Internet users telling them how to kill the worm and prevent it from infecting more computers. Morris was convicted of a federal felony and sentenced to three years probation, 400 hours of community service, and $10,050 in fines.

With the release of the Morris Worm, a group of computer experts from the National Computer Security Center, part of the National Security Agency, gathered to discuss the susceptibility of Internet-connected computers to attack. Out of these meetings, the Computer Emergency Response Team Coordination Center, a federally funded organization that monitors and reports activity on the Internet, was started at Carnegie Mellon University. This is considered the beginning of Internet security.

THE JOB

The duties of an Internet security specialist vary depending on where he or she works, how big the company is, and the degree of sensitivity of the information that is being protected. The duties are also affected by whether the specialist is a consultant or works in-house.

Internet security usually falls under the jurisdiction of a systems engineering or systems administration department. A large company that deals with sensitive information probably has one or two Internet security specialists who devote all of their time and energy to Internet security. Many firms, upon connecting to the Internet, give security duties to the person who is in charge of systems administration. A smaller firm might hire an Internet security specialist to come in and set them up with security systems and software.

A *firewall* is a system set up to act as a barrier of protection between the outside world of the Internet and the company. A specialist can tell the firewall to limit access or permit access to users. The Internet security specialist does this by configuring it to define the kind of access to allow or restrict.

Primarily, Internet security specialists are in charge of monitoring the flow of information through the firewall. Security specialists must be able to write code and configure the software to alert them when certain kinds of activities occur. They can tell the program what activity to allow and what to disallow. They can even program the software to page them or send them an email if some questionable activity occurs. Logs are kept of all access to the network. Security specialists monitor the logs and watch for anything out of the ordinary. If they see something strange, they must make a judgment call as to whether the activity was innocent or malicious. Then they must investigate and do some detective work—perhaps even tracking down the user who initiated the action. In other instances, they might have to create a new program to prevent that action from happening again.

Sometimes the Internet security specialist is in charge of virus protection or encryption and user authentication systems. *Viruses* are programs written with the express purpose of harming a hard drive and can enter a network through email attachments or infected CD-ROMs. Encryption and authentication are used with any network activity that requires transmission of delicate information, such as passwords, user accounts, or even credit card numbers.

Type of Security Technologies Used

The Computer Security Institute, in cooperation with the San Francisco Federal Bureau of Investigation's Computer Intrusion Squad, conducts an annual survey of security practitioners in U.S. corporations, government agencies, universities, medical institutions, and financial institutions. Security practitioners reported using the following security technologies:

Firewalls	98 percent
Anti-virus software	97 percent
Anti-spyware software	79 percent
Server-based access control lists	70 percent
Intrusion detection systems	69 percent
Encryption for data in transit	63 percent
Encryption for data in storage	48 percent
Reusable account/login passwords	46 percent
Intrusion prevention systems	43 percent
Log management software	41 percent
Application-level firewall	39 percent
Smart cards/one-time password tokens	38 percent
Forensic tools	38 percent
Public key infrastructure	36 percent
Specialized wireless security system	32 percent
Endpoint security client software	31 percent
Biometrics	20 percent

Source: *2006 CSI/FBI Computer Crime & Security Survey*, Computer Security Institute

Secondary duties can include security administrative work, such as establishing security policies for the company, or security engineering duties, which are more technical in nature. For example, some companies might deal with such sensitive information that the company forbids any of its information to be transmitted over email. Programs can be written to disallow transmission of any company product information or to alert the specialist when this sensitive information is transmitted. The security specialist also might be in charge of educating employees on security policies concerning their network.

Internet security consultants have a different set of duties. Consultants are primarily in charge of designing and implementing solutions to their clients' security problems. They must be able to listen to and detect the needs of the client and then meet their needs. They perform routine assessments to determine if there are insecurities within the clients' network and, if there are, find ways to correct them. A company might employ a consultant as a preventive measure to avoid attacks. Other times, a consultant might be called on after a security breach has been detected to find the problem, fix it, and even track down the perpetrator.

Secondary duties of an Internet security consultant include management and administrative duties. He or she manages various accounts and must be able to track them and maintain paperwork and communications. Senior consultants have consultants who report to them and take on supervisory responsibilities in addition to their primary duties.

A benefit of using consultants is bringing new perspectives to an old problem. Often, they can use their many experiences with other clients to help find solutions. The consultant does not work solely with one client but has multiple accounts. He or she spends a lot of time traveling and must be reachable at a moment's notice.

REQUIREMENTS

High School

If you are a high school student and think you want to get into the Internet security industry, first and foremost you need to get involved in computer science/programming classes. Don't just book learn, however. Hands-on experience is key and probably is what will get you your first job. Spend time in the school computer lab, learn how computers work, and dabble with the latest technologies. Most of those employed in the field today began at a young age just playing around. What began as a hobby eventually turned into an enjoyable and challenging career.

If you are interested in management or consulting, a well-rounded educational background is important. You should take classes in mathematics, science, and English. You may also want to take business classes to become familiar with the business world.

Postsecondary Training

College courses show employers that you have what it takes to learn. However, most colleges do not have specific programs in Internet security. Most offer computer science, networking, and programming-related degrees, which are highly recommended. Computer lab courses teach how to work with a team to solve problems and complete assignments—something that you will probably do in this field—especially in the consulting business. Programming requires an understanding of mathematics and algorithms. Law enforcement classes are also beneficial. By learning the mindset of the criminal, you can better protect your client or employer. Last, being versed in intellectual property law is important because you will be working with transmitting and protecting sensitive information as it travels to various locations.

Internships are the best way to gain hands-on experience. They offer real-life situations and protected work environments where you can see what Internet security is all about. Internships are not common, however, mostly because of security problems that arise from bringing inexperienced young people into contact with sensitive, confidential information. The majority of exposed hackers are under 20 years of age so it is easy to understand companies' unwillingness to offer internships.

On-the-job training is the best way to break into Internet security. Without experience, you can never land a job in the field.

Certification or Licensing

The International Webmasters Association offers a voluntary certification program for Internet security specialists. Certification is also available from the Information Systems Security Certification Consortium and various vendors of Internet security software and other products. Each vendor offers its own training and certification program, which varies from company to company. Some certifications can be completed in a matter of a few days; others take years. The majority of those employed in the field are not certified; however, certification is a trend and is considered an advantage. The more certifications you have, the more you have to offer a company.

The Internet is constantly evolving, and Internet technology changes so rapidly that it is vital for the Internet security specialist to stay on top of current technology. After all, if a hacker has knowledge of cutting edge technology and can use it to break into a system, the security specialist must be trained to counter those attacks. Security specialists must be well versed in the same cutting-edge technology. Often, the vendor creating the most current technology is the best training source. In the future, the technology is likely to become more complex, and so is the training. Ideally, product certification coupled with a few years of hands-on experience qualifies you for advancement.

Other Requirements

If you like doing the same thing on a daily basis (like monitoring network activity logs and writing code), a job as Internet security specialist might be good for you. On the other hand, you must be flexible so that you are ready to meet each new challenge with fresh ideas. Some hackers are creative, and it is important that the security specialist be just as creative.

It is not uncommon for those applying for security positions to have background checks or at least have their list of references closely interviewed to make sure the applicants are trustworthy. In fact, many companies prefer to hire individuals who have been recommended to them directly by someone they know and trust.

Consultants must be well organized because they work with many accounts at once. Communication skills are important because consultants often deal with management and try to sell them on the importance of security software. They must also be willing to travel on a regular basis to visit their accounts.

EXPLORING

If Internet security interests you, play around on your computer. Check out programming books from the local library and learn how to write simple code. You might also want to read professional publications such as *Computer Security Journal,* which is published by the Computer Security Institute (http://www.gocsi.com), and *Information Security* magazine, which is published by TechTarget (http://www.infosecuritymag.com). Another publication to consider is the quarterly magazine *2600* (http://www.2600.com). While *2600* is aimed at hackers, reading the articles will give you an understanding of how some systems are broken into and help you develop your ability to think of defenses.

High school science clubs and competitions allow you to experiment with computer programming. They are great places to design and implement systems and solutions in a nonthreatening atmosphere. You can also work with other students to get accustomed to working in teams.

The most obvious place to learn about the Internet is on the Internet. Surf the Web and research the many security issues facing users today. Visit the sites of consulting firms where you can get an idea of the services these firms offer.

National news magazines, newspapers, and trade magazines are good sources of information. You can also find out a lot about current trends and hiring practices. Classified sections reveal what kind of market there is for security specialists and where the jobs are.

EMPLOYERS

Any company with an Internet presence (Web site, FTP site, email service, etc.) has the potential for security breaches and can benefit from the work and advice of an Internet security specialist. Depending on the size of the company and the nature of the company's business, it might use outside consultants or employ one part-time or several full-time employees.

An obvious place of employment is an Internet security consulting firm. Some business consulting firms like Ernst & Young are adding Internet security branches to their current businesses.

Data forensics is another growing business where Internet security specialists are hired to act as detectives to find culprits who break into computer networks. To fight this type of crime, the Federal Bureau of Investigation has set up a National Infrastructure Protection Center at its headquarters and Regional Computer Intrusion Squads in selected field offices throughout the United States.

STARTING OUT

It is unlikely that someone fresh out of high school or college will get a job as an Internet security specialist. Although education is important, experience is key in the field. Certifications are beneficial, but again, they do not mean much without experience. An internship in systems administration or engineering might introduce you to the security issues of that company.

Many who are in Internet security began in PC technical support and moved to systems administration or engineering. These jobs often include security responsibilities that then lead to positions focusing primarily on security.

If word-of-mouth doesn't get you a job, check the classifieds—both in the local newspapers and trade magazines. Many places post job openings on their Web sites.

ADVANCEMENT

Internet security specialists can move into supervisory or management positions and sometimes into executive positions. Those who work for small companies can sometimes advance by moving to larger firms with more sensitive data and more complicated security issues. With experience, an Internet security specialist can become a consultant.

Internet security consultants can become *sneakers* or part of a *tiger team*. Sneakers and tiger teams are the best in the field who are called in to crack a system on purpose in order to find security holes and then patch them.

EARNINGS

The field of Internet security is a lucrative business and the salary potential is growing. Internet security specialists are among the highest paid of all information technology professionals. An entry-level specialist can expect to earn $40,000 to $50,000. According to a survey by Robert Half Technology, systems security administrators earned salaries that ranged from $70,500 to $99,750 or more in 2007. According to *Computerworld*'s 2006 Salary Survey, Internet security specialists had average salaries (including bonuses) of $81,968 in 2006.

Salaries increase with the size of the company and the nature of the information specialists are charged with protecting. Specialists working with extremely confidential information in an industry (such as the automotive industry) will receive higher pay than those working at a small family business. The highest paying industries are manufacturing, computers, and communication/utilities companies. Military and government sectors pay the least.

Benefits for full-time employees may include paid vacation, paid sick days, personal days, medical and dental insurance, and bonuses.

WORK ENVIRONMENT

Because Internet security specialists work with computers and computers require a controlled atmosphere, the work environment is typically indoors in a well-lit, climate-controlled office. Security specialists can expect to spend many hours sitting in front of a computer screen using a keyboard. Work is generally done alone, although a consultant might train an in-house person on how to use certain software.

Most work schedules require 40 to 50 hours a week. Consultants travel frequently, and their work schedules do not necessarily follow typical nine-to-five working hours. There are instances where additional hours are required—for example, if a serious breach of security is detected and time is of the essence to fix it. It is not uncommon for employees to be on call so they can respond quickly to critical situations.

Although this line of work might seem stressful, it generally is not. Most businesses see the value of protecting their information and budget appropriately for the necessary tools, equipment, and staff.

OUTLOOK

Employment for Internet security specialists will grow faster than the average for all occupations. The number of companies with a presence on the Internet is growing rapidly. As these companies connect their private networks to the public Internet, they will need to protect their confidential information. Currently, the demand for Internet security specialists is greater than the supply, and this trend is expected to continue as the number of businesses connecting to the Internet continues to grow.

Until now, most Internet security specialists have gotten by with general skills. In the future, however, they will need more specialized skills and certification. Staying on top of current technologies will be one of the biggest challenges.

Because of the ever-changing new technology, educational institutions will continue to have difficulty in training students for this field. Vendors and on-the-job experience will continue to provide the best training.

FOR MORE INFORMATION

A federally funded organization, the CERT Coordination Center studies, monitors, and publishes security-related activity and research. They also provide an incident response service to those who have been hacked.

CERT Coordination Center
Software Engineering Institute
Carnegie Mellon University
Pittsburgh, PA 15213-3890
Tel: 412-268-7090
Email: cert@cert.org
http://www.cert.org

*A professional organization for information security professionals,
CSI provides education and training for its members.*
Computer Security Institute (CSI)
600 Harrison Street
San Francisco, CA 94107-1387
http://www.gocsi.com

For information on certification, contact
Information Systems Security Certification Consortium
1964 Gallows Road, Suite 210
Vienna, VA 22182-3814
Tel: 866-462-4777
https://www.isc2.org

Visit the IWA's Web site for information on its voluntary certification program.
International Webmasters Association (IWA)
119 East Union Street, Suite F
Pasadena, CA 91103-3952
Tel: 626-449-3709
http://www.iwanet.org

Quality Assurance Testers

QUICK FACTS

School Subjects
Computer science
Mathematics

Personal Skills
Mechanical/manipulative
Technical/scientific

Work Environment
Primarily indoors
Primarily one location

Minimum Education Level
High school diploma

Salary Range
$17,990 to $51,690 to
$83,719+

Certification or Licensing
Voluntary

Outlook
Faster than the average

DOT
033

GOE
08.02.03

NOC
2233

O*NET-SOC
51-9061.00

OVERVIEW

Quality assurance testers examine new or modified computer software applications to evaluate whether or not they perform as intended. Testers might also verify that computer-automated quality assurance programs function properly. Their work entails trying to crash computer programs by punching in certain characters very quickly, for example, or by clicking the mouse on the border of an icon. They keep very close track of the combinations they enter so that they can replicate the situation if the program does crash. They also offer opinions on the user-friendliness of the program. They report in detail any problems they find or suggestions they have both verbally and in writing to supervisors.

HISTORY

The first major advances in modern computer technology were made during World War II. After the war, it was thought that the enormous size of computers, which easily took up the space of entire warehouses, would limit their use to huge government projects. Accordingly, the 1950 census was computer processed.

The introduction of semiconductors to computer technology made possible smaller and less expensive computers. Businesses began adapting computers to their operations as early as 1954. Within 30 years, computers had revolutionized the way people work, play, and shop. Today, computers are everywhere, from businesses of all kinds to government agencies, charitable organizations, and private homes. Over the years, the technology has continued to shrink computer size as their speeds have increased at an unprecedented rate.

Engineers have been able to significantly increase the memory capacity and processing speed of computer hardware. These technological advances enable computers to effectively process more information than ever before. Consequently, more sophisticated software applications have been created. These programs offer extremely user-friendly and sophisticated working environments that would not have been possible on older, slower computers. In addition, the introduction of CD-ROMs and DVD-ROMs to the mass computer market enabled the production of complex programs stored on compact discs.

As software applications became more complicated, the probability and sheer number of errors increased. Quality assurance departments were expanded to develop methods for testing software applications for errors, or "bugs." Quality assurance is now a branch of science and engineering in its own right. "Testing is finally being recognized as an important phase of the product cycle," says Steve Devinney, a senior consultant at the Quality Assurance Institute in Orlando, Florida. The importance of good testing procedures came to the forefront of the computer industry in the late 1990s with the emergence of the Year 2000 (Y2K) problems. "Testers were second-class citizens," says Devinney. "The thought was that if the project was running late, you could just skip the testing. Now, because of the Y2K situation, testing has become more important."

The field has changed with the advent of automated testing tools. As technology continues to advance, many quality assurance tests are automated. Quality assurance testers also "test the tests," that is, look for errors in the programs that test the software. There will always be a need for quality assurance testers, however, since they, not another computer, are best suited to judge a program from a user's point of view. "The use of tools will increase, but they can never replace humans," notes Devinney.

THE JOB

Before manufacturers can introduce a product on the consumer market, they must run extensive tests on its safety and quality. Failing to do so thoroughly can be very expensive, resulting in liability lawsuits when unsafe products harm people or in poor sales when products do not perform well. The nature and scope of quality assurance testing varies greatly. High-tech products, such as computers and other electronics, require extremely detailed technical testing.

Computer software applications undergo a specific series of tests designed to anticipate and help solve problems that users might encounter. Quality assurance testers examine new or modified computer software applications to evaluate whether or not they function at the desired level. They also verify that computer automated quality assurance programs perform in accordance with designer specifications and user requirements. This includes checking the product's functionality (how it will work), network performance (how it will work with other products), installation (how to put it in), and configuration (how it is set up).

Some quality assurance testers spend most of their time working on software programs or playing computer games, just as an average consumer might. If it is a game, for example, they play it over and over again for hours, trying to make moves quickly or slowly to "crash" it. A program crashes if it completely stops functioning due to, among other things, an inability to process incoming commands. For other types of programs, such as word processors, quality assurance testers might intentionally make errors, type very quickly, or click the mouse on inappropriate areas of the screen to see if the program can correctly handle such usage.

Quality assurance testers keep detailed records of the hours logged working on individual programs. They write reports based on their observations about how well the program performed in different situations, always imagining how typical, nontechnical users would judge it. The goal is to make the programs more efficient, user-friendly, fun, and visually exciting. Lastly, they keep track of the precise combinations of keystrokes and mouse clicks that made the program crash. This type of record is very important because it enables supervisors and programmers to replicate the problem. Then they can better isolate its source and begin to design a solution.

Programs to be tested arrive in the quality assurance department after programmers and software engineers have finished the initial version. Each program is assigned a specific number of tests, and the quality assurance testers go to work. They make sure that the correct tests are run, write reports, and send the program back to the programmers for revisions and correction. Some testers have direct contact with the programmers. After evaluating a product, they might meet with programmers to describe the problems they encountered and suggest ways for solving glitches. Others report solely to a quality assurance supervisor.

When automated tests are to be run, quality assurance testers tell the computer which tests to administer and then ensure that they run smoothly by watching a computer screen for interruption codes and breakdown signals. They also interpret test results, verifying their credibility by running them through special programs that check for

A quality assurance tester uses an electron microscope to examine the surface of a 200-mm wafer. *(Matthias Rietschel, AP Images)*

accuracy and reliability. Then, they write reports explaining their conclusions.

Some quality assurance testers have direct contact with users experiencing problems with their software. They listen closely to customer complaints to determine the precise order of keystrokes that led to the problem. Then, they attempt to duplicate the problem on their own computers and run in-depth tests to figure out the cause. Eventually, if the problem is not simply a result of user error, they inform programmers and software engineers of the problems and suggest certain paths to take in resolving them.

Quality assurance testers with solid work experience and bachelor's degrees in a computer-related field might go on to work as *quality assurance analysts*. Analysts write and revise the quality standards for each software program that passes through the department. They also use computer programming skills to create the tests and programs the quality assurance testers use to test the programs. They might evaluate proposals for new software applications, advising management about whether or not the program will be able to achieve its goals. Since they know many software applications inside and out, they might also train users on how to work with various programs.

REQUIREMENTS
High School
Interested in becoming a quality assurance tester? If so, then take as many computer classes as possible to become familiar with how

to effectively operate computer software and hardware. Math and science courses are very helpful for teaching the necessary analytical skills. English and speech classes will help you improve your verbal and written communication skills, which are also essential to the success of quality assurance testers.

Postsecondary Training

It is debatable whether or not a bachelor's degree is necessary to become a quality assurance tester. Some companies require a bachelor's degree in computer science, while others prefer people who come from the business sector who have a small amount of computer experience because they best match the technical level of the software's typical users. If testers are interested in advancement, however, a bachelor's degree is almost a mandate.

Few universities or colleges offer courses on quality assurance testing. As a result, most companies offer in-house training on how to test their particular products.

Certification or Licensing

As the information technology industry becomes more competitive, the necessity for management to be able to distinguish professional and skilled individuals in the field becomes mandatory, according to the Quality Assurance Institute (QAI). Certification demonstrates a level of understanding in carrying out relevant principles and practices, and provides a common ground for communication among professionals in the field of software quality. The organization offers the designations certified software tester, certified software quality analyst, certified software project manager, certified manager of software testing, and certified manager of software quality.

Other Requirements

Quality assurance testers need superior verbal and written communication skills. They also must show a proficiency in critical and analytical thinking and be able to critique something diplomatically. Quality assurance testers should have an eye for detail, be focused, and have a lot of enthusiasm because sometimes the work is monotonous and repetitive. Testers should definitely enjoy the challenge of breaking the system.

Some companies recommend testers have some programming skills in languages such as C, C++, SQL, or Visual Basic. Others prefer testers with no programming ability. "The most important thing is that testers understand the business and the testing tools with which they are working," says Steve Devinney. "You have to be a good problem-solver and detective. Testing is a difficult job."

EXPLORING

Students interested in quality assurance and other computer jobs should gain wide exposure to computer systems and programs of all kinds. Get a computer at home, borrow a friend's, or check out the computer lab at your school. Work on becoming comfortable using the Windows programs and learn how to operate all parts of your computer, including the hardware, thoroughly. Look for bugs in your software at home and practice writing them up. Keep up with emerging technologies. If you cannot get hands-on experiences, read about them. Join a computer group or society. Read books on testing and familiarize yourself with methodology, terminology, the development cycle, and where testing fits in. Subscribe to newsletters or magazines related to testing or quality assurance. Get involved with online newsgroups that deal with the subject. Check Web sites that deal with quality assurance.

If you live in an area where numerous computer software companies are located, you might be able to secure a part-time or summer job as a quality assurance tester. In addition, investigate the possibility of spending an afternoon with an employed quality assurance tester to find out what a typical day is like for him or her.

EMPLOYERS

Quality assurance testers are employed throughout the United States. Opportunities are best in large cities and suburbs where business and industry are active. Many work for software manufacturers, a cluster of which are located in Silicon Valley, in northern California. There are also concentrations of software manufacturers in Boston, Chicago, and Atlanta.

STARTING OUT

Positions in the field of quality assurance can be obtained several different ways. Many universities and colleges host computer job fairs on campus throughout the year that include representatives from several hardware and software companies. Internships and summer jobs with such corporations are always beneficial and provide experience that will give you the edge over your competition. General computer job fairs are also held throughout the year in larger cities. Some job openings are advertised in newspapers. There are many career sites on the World Wide Web that post job openings, salary surveys, and current employment trends. The Web also has online publications that deal specifically with quality assurance. You can also obtain information from associations for quality professionals, such as the QAI, and from computer organizations, including the IEEE Computer Society.

ADVANCEMENT

Quality assurance testers are considered entry-level positions in some companies. After acquiring more experience and technical knowledge, testers might become quality assurance analysts, who write and revise the quality assurance standards or specifications for new programs. They also create the quality assurance examinations that testers use to evaluate programs. This usually involves using computer programming. Some analysts also evaluate proposals for new software products to decide whether the proposed product is capable of doing what it is supposed to do. Analysts are sometimes promoted to quality assurance manager positions, which require some knowledge of software coding, the entire software production process, and test automation. They manage quality assurance teams for specific software products before and beyond their release.

Some testers also go on to become programmers or software engineers.

EARNINGS

Software quality assurance testers earned salaries that ranged from less than $40,816 to $83,719 or more annually in 2007, according to Salary.com. Workers with many years of technical and management experience can earn higher salaries. Testers in all industries had earnings that ranged from less than $17,990 to $51,690 or more annually in 2006, according to the U.S. Department of Labor. Testers generally receive a full benefits package as well, including health insurance, paid vacation, and sick leave. As in many industries, people with advanced degrees have the potential to make the most money.

WORK ENVIRONMENT

Quality assurance testers work in computer labs or offices. The work is generally repetitive and even monotonous. If a game is being tested, for example, a tester may have to play it for hours until it finally crashes, if at all. This might seem like great fun, but most testers agree that even the newest, most exciting game loses its appeal after several hours. This aspect of the job proves to be very frustrating and boring for some individuals.

Since quality assurance work involves keeping very detailed records, the job can also be stressful. For example, if a tester works on a word processing program for several hours, he or she must be able to recall at any moment the last few keystrokes entered in case the program crashes. This requires long periods of concentration, which can be tiring. Monitoring computer screens to make sure automated quality assurance tests are running properly often has the same effect.

Meeting with supervisors, programmers, and engineers to discuss ideas for software projects can be intellectually stimulating. At these times, testers should feel at ease communicating with superiors. On the other end, testers who field customer complaints on the telephone may be forced to bear the brunt of customer dissatisfaction, an almost certain source of stress.

Quality assurance testers generally work regular, 40-hour weeks. During the final stages before a program goes into mass production and packaging, however, testers are frequently called on to work overtime.

OUTLOOK

Employment for quality assurance testers is expected to grow faster than the average for all occupations over the next decade. This trend is predicted despite an increasing level of quality assurance automation. Before, software companies were able to make big profits by being the first to introduce a specific kind of product, such as a word processor or presentation kit, to the marketplace. Now, with so many versions of similar software on the market, competition is forcing firms to focus their energies on customer service. Many companies, therefore, aim to perfect their software applications before they hit the shelves. Searching for every small program glitch in this way requires the effort of many quality assurance testers.

This same push toward premarket perfection helps to explain the development of more accurate and efficient quality assurance automation. To stay competitive, companies must refine their quality assurance procedures to ever-higher levels. "In the next few years, testing will begin on Day One of the project," says Steve Devinney. "This means that testers will be involved in the process from the beginning because they are the ones who know what the product's functionality should be. Without testing requirements, you cannot do anything."

FOR MORE INFORMATION

For information on scholarships, student membership, and to read Careers in Computer Science and Computer Engineering, *visit the IEEE's Web site:*

IEEE Computer Society
1730 Massachusetts Avenue, NW
Washington, DC 20036-1992
Tel: 202-371-0101
Email: membership@computer.org
http://www.computer.org

For career advice and industry information, contact
International Game Developers Association
19 Mantua Road
Mt. Royal, NJ 08061-1006
Tel: 856-423-2990
Email: contact@igda.org
http://www.igda.org

For information on certification, contact
Quality Assurance Institute
2101 Park Center Drive, Suite 200
Orlando, FL 32835-7614
Tel: 407-363-1111
Email: info@qaiworldwide.com
http://www.qaiworldwide.org

For industry information, contact the following organizations:
Software & Information Industry Association
1090 Vermont Avenue, NW, Sixth Floor
Washington, DC 20005-4095
Tel: 202-289-7442
http://www.siia.net

Software Testing Institute
http://www.softwaretestinginstitute.com

Software Designers

OVERVIEW

Software designers are responsible for creating new ideas and designing prepackaged and customized computer software. Software designers devise applications such as word processors, front-end database programs, and spreadsheet programs that make it possible for computers to complete given tasks and to solve problems. Once a need in the market has been identified, software designers first conceive of the program on a global level by outlining what the program will do. Then they write the specifications from which programmers code computer commands to perform the given functions.

HISTORY

"In 1983, software development exploded with the introduction of the personal computer. Standard applications included not only spreadsheets and word processors, but graphics packages and communications systems," according to "Events in the History of Computing," compiled by the Institute of Electrical and Electronics Engineers (IEEE) Computer Society.

Advances in computer technology have enabled professionals to put computers to work in a range of activities once thought impossible. Computer software designers have been able to take advantage of computer hardware improvements in speed, memory capacity, reliability, and accuracy to create programs to do almost anything. With the extensive proliferation of computers in our society, there is a great market for user-friendly, imaginative, and high-performance software. Business and industry rely heavily on the power of computers and use both prepackaged software and software that has been

QUICK FACTS

School Subjects
Computer science
Mathematics

Personal Skills
Communication/ideas
Technical/scientific

Work Environment
Primarily indoors
Primarily one location

Minimum Education Level
Bachelor's degree

Salary Range
$51,070 to $93,950 to $160,000+

Certification or Licensing
Voluntary

Outlook
Much faster than the average

DOT
030

GOE
02.07.01

NOC
2173

O*NET-SOC
15-1011.00

custom-designed for their own specific use. Also, with more people purchasing computer systems for home use, the retail market for prepackaged software has grown steadily. Given these conditions, computer software designing will be an important field in the industry for years to come.

The software industry has many facets, including packaged applications for personal computers (known as "shrink-wrapped software"); operating systems for stand-alone and networked systems; management tools for networks; enterprise software that enables efficient management of large corporations' production, sales, and information systems; software applications and operating systems for mainframe computers; and customized software for specific industry management.

Packaged software is written for mass distribution, not for the specific needs of a particular user. Broad categories include operating systems, utilities, applications, and programming languages. Operating systems control the basic functions of a computer or network. Utilities perform support functions, such as backup or virus protection. Programming software is used to develop the sets of instructions that build all other types of software. The software familiar to most computer users is called application software. This category includes word-processing, spreadsheets, and email packages, commonly used in business, as well as games and reference software used in homes, and subject- or skill-based software used in schools.

THE JOB

Without software, computer hardware would have nothing to do. Computers need to be told exactly what to do, and software is the set of codes that gives the computer those instructions. It comes in the form of the familiar prepackaged software that you find in a computer store, such as games, word processing, spreadsheet, and desktop publishing programs, and in customized applications designed to fit specific needs of a particular business. Software designers are the initiators of these complex programs. Computer programmers then create the software by writing the code that carries out the directives of the designer.

Software designers must envision every detail of what an application will do, how it will do it, and how it will look (the user interface). A simple example is how a home accounting program is created. The software designer first lays out the overall functionality of the program, specifying what it should be able to do, such as balancing a checkbook, keeping track of incoming and outgoing bills, and maintaining records of expenses. For each of these tasks, the software designer will outline the design details for the specific functions that he or she has mandated, such as what menus and icons will be used, what each screen will look like, and whether there will be help or dialog boxes to assist the user. For example, the designer may specify that the expense record part of the program produce a pie chart that shows the percentage of each household expense in the overall household budget. The designer can specify that the program automatically display the pie chart each time a budget assessment is completed or only after the user clicks on the appropriate icon on the toolbar.

Some software companies specialize in building custom-designed software. This software is highly specialized for specific needs or problems of particular businesses. Some businesses are large enough that they employ in-house software designers who create software applications for their computer systems. A related field is software engineering, which involves writing customized complex software to solve specific engineering or technical problems of a business or industry.

Whether the designer is working on a mass-market or a custom application, the first step is to define the overall goals for the application. This is typically done in consultation with management if working at a software supply company, or with the client if working on a custom-designed project. Then, the software designer studies the goals and problems of the project. If working on custom-designed software, the designer must also take into consideration the

Books to Read: History of Computing

Campbell-Kelly, Martin. *From Airline Reservations to Sonic the Hedgehog: A History of the Software Industry.* Cambridge, Mass.: The MIT Press, 2004.

Ceruzzi, Paul E. *A History of Modern Computing.* 2d ed. Cambridge, Mass.: The MIT Press, 2003.

Frauenfelder, Mark. *The Computer: An Illustrated History.* London, U.K.: Carlton Publishing Group, 2007.

Ifrah, Georges. *The Universal History of Computing: From the Abacus to the Quantum Computer.* Hoboken, N.J.: Wiley, 2002.

Levy, Steven. *Hackers: Heroes of the Computer Revolution.* New York: Penguin Putnam, 2001.

Linzmayer, Owen. *Apple Confidential 2.0: The Definitive History of the World's Most Colorful Company.* 2d ed. San Francisco: No Starch Press, 2004.

Raum, Elizabeth. *The History of the Computer (Inventions That Changed the World).* Portsmouth, N.H.: Heinemann, 2007.

existing computer system of the client. Next, the software designer works on the program strategy and specific design detail that he or she has envisioned. At this point, the designer may need to write a proposal outlining the design and estimating time and cost allocations. Based on this report, management or the client decides if the project should proceed.

Once approval is given, the software designer and the programmers begin working on writing the software program. Typically, the software designer writes the specifications for the program, and the applications programmers write the programming codes.

In addition to the duties involved in design, a software designer may be responsible for writing a user's manual or at least writing a report for what should be included in the user's manual. After testing and debugging the program, the software designer will present it to management or to the client.

REQUIREMENTS

High School

If you are interested in computer science, you should take as many computer, math, and science courses as possible; they provide fundamental math and computer knowledge and teach analytical thinking skills. Classes that focus on schematic drawing and flowcharts are also very valuable. English and speech courses will help you improve your communication skills, which are very important to software designers who must make formal presentations to management and clients. Also, many technical/vocational schools offer programs in software programming and design. The qualities developed by these classes, plus imagination and an ability to work well under pressure, are key to success in software design.

Postsecondary Training

A bachelor's degree in computer science plus one year's experience with a programming language is required for most software designers.

In the past, the computer industry has tended to be pretty flexible about official credentials; demonstrated computer proficiency and work experience have often been enough to obtain a good position. However, as more people enter the field, competition has increased, and job requirements have become more stringent. Technical knowledge alone does not suffice in the field of software design anymore. In order to be a successful software designer, you should have at least a peripheral knowledge of the field for which you intend to design software, such as business, education, or science. Individuals with degrees in education and subsequent teaching experience are much sought after as designers for educational software. Those with bachelor's degrees in computer science with a minor in business or accounting have an excellent chance for employment in designing business or accounting software.

Certification or Licensing

Certification in software development is offered by companies such as Sun Microsystems, Hewlett-Packard, IBM, Novell, and Oracle. While not required, certification tells employers that your skills meet industry education and training standards.

Additionally, the Institute of Electrical and Electronics Engineers Computer Society offers the designation of certified software development professional to individuals who have a bachelor's degree, a minimum of 9,000 hours of software engineering experience within at least six of 11 knowledge areas, and pass an examination.

Other Requirements

Software design is project- and detail-oriented, and therefore, you must be patient and diligent. You must also enjoy problem-solving challenges and be able to work under a deadline with minimal supervision. As a software designer, you should also possess good communication skills for consulting both with management and with clients who will have varying levels of technical expertise.

Software companies are looking for individuals with vision and imagination to help them create new and exciting programs to sell in the ever-competitive software market. Superior technical skills and knowledge combined with motivation, imagination, and exuberance will make you an attractive candidate.

EXPLORING

Spending a day with a professional software designer or applications programmer will allow you to experience firsthand what this work entails. School guidance counselors can often help you organize such a meeting.

If you are interested in computer industry careers in general, you should learn as much as possible about computers. Keep up with new technology by talking to other computer users and by reading related magazines, such as *Computer* (http://www.computer.org/computer). You will also find it helpful to join computer clubs and use online services and the Internet to find more information about this field.

Advanced students can put their design ideas and programming knowledge to work by designing and programming their own applications, such as simple games and utility programs.

EMPLOYERS

Software designers are employed throughout the United States. Opportunities are best in large cities and suburbs where business and industry are active. Programmers who develop software systems work for software manufacturers, many of whom are in Silicon Valley, in northern California. There are also concentrations of software manufacturers in Boston, Chicago, and Atlanta, among other places. Designers who adapt and tailor the software to meet specific needs of end-users work for those end-user companies, many of which are scattered across the country.

STARTING OUT

Software design positions are regarded as some of the most interesting, and therefore the most competitive, in the computer industry. Some software designers are promoted from an entry-level programming position. Software design positions in software supply companies and large custom software companies will be difficult to secure straight out of college or technical/vocational school.

Entry-level programming and design jobs may be listed in the help wanted sections of newspapers. Employment agencies and online job banks are other good sources.

Students in technical schools or universities should take advantage of the campus career services office. They should check regularly for internship postings, job listings, and notices of on-campus recruitment. Career services offices are also valuable resources for resume tips and interviewing techniques. Internships and summer jobs with such corporations are always beneficial and provide experience that will give you the edge over your competition. General computer job fairs are also held throughout the year in larger cities.

There are many career sites on the World Wide Web that post job openings, salary surveys, and current employment trends. The Web also has online publications that deal specifically with computer jobs. You can also obtain information from computer organizations such as the IEEE Computer Society. Because this is such a competitive field, you will need to show initiative and creativity that will set you apart from other applicants.

ADVANCEMENT

In general, programmers work between one and five years before being promoted to software designer. A programmer can move up by demonstrating an ability to create new software ideas that translate well into marketable applications. Individuals with a knack for spotting trends in the software market are also likely to advance.

Those software designers who demonstrate leadership may be promoted to *project team leader*. Project team leaders are responsible for developing new software projects and overseeing the work done by software designers and applications programmers. With experience as a project team leader, a motivated software designer may be promoted to a position as a *software manager* who runs projects from an even higher level.

EARNINGS

Salaries for software designers vary with the size of the company and by location. Salaries may be slightly higher in areas where there is a large concentration of computer companies, such as the Silicon Valley in northern California and parts of Washington, Oregon, and the East Coast.

The National Association of Colleges and Employers reports that average starting salaries for graduates with a doctoral degree in computer science were $93,050 in 2005. Graduates with a bachelor's degree in computer science averaged $51,070 in 2007.

Median salaries for computer and information scientists (which include software designers) were $93,950 in 2006, according to the U.S. Department of Labor. Salaries ranged from less than $53,590 to $144,880 or more annually. At the managerial level, salaries are even higher and can reach $160,000 or more. Most designers work for large companies, which offer a full benefits package that includes health insurance, vacation and sick time, and a profit sharing or retirement plan.

WORK ENVIRONMENT

Software designers work in comfortable environments. Many computer companies are known for their casual work atmosphere; employees generally do not have to wear suits, except during client meetings. Overall, software designers work standard weeks. However, they may be required to work overtime near a deadline. It is common in software design to share office or cubicle space with two or three coworkers, which is typical of the team approach to working. As a software designer or applications programmer, much of the day is spent in front of the computer, although a software designer will have occasional team meetings or meetings with clients.

Software design can be stressful work for several reasons. First, the market for software is very competitive and companies are pushing to develop more innovative software and to get it on the market before competitors do. For this same reason, software design is also very exciting and creative work. Second, software designers are given a project and a deadline. It is up to the designer and team members to budget their time to finish in the allocated time. Finally, working with programming languages and so many details can be very frustrating, especially when the tiniest glitch means the program will not run. For this reason, software designers must be patient and diligent.

OUTLOOK

Employment in software design is expected to grow much faster than the average for all occupations through 2014, according to the *Occupational Outlook Handbook*. Employment will increase as technology becomes more sophisticated and organizations continue to adopt and integrate these technologies, making for plentiful job openings. Hardware designers and systems programmers are constantly developing faster, more powerful, and more user-friendly hardware and operating systems. As long as these advancements continue, the industry will need software designers to create software to use these improvements.

Business may have less need to contract for custom software as more prepackaged software arrives on the market that allows users with minimal computer skills to "build" their own software using components that they customize. However, the growth in the retail software market is expected to make up for this loss in customized services.

The expanding integration of Internet technologies by businesses has resulted in a rising demand for a variety of skilled professionals who can develop and support a variety of Internet applications.

FOR MORE INFORMATION

For information on internships, student membership, and the student magazine Crossroads, *contact*
Association for Computing Machinery
1515 Broadway
New York, NY 10036-8901
Tel: 800-342-6626
Email: SIGS@acm.org
http://www.acm.org

For information on career opportunities for women in computing, *contact*

Association for Women in Computing
41 Sutter Street, Suite 1006
San Francisco, CA 94104-5414
Tel: 415-905-4663
Email: info@awc-hq.org
http://www.awc-hq.org

For information on scholarships, certification, student membership, *and to read* Careers in Computer Science and Computer Engineering, *visit the IEEE's Web site:*

IEEE Computer Society
1730 Massachusetts Avenue, NW
Washington, DC 20036-1992
Tel: 202-371-0101
Email: membership@computer.org
http://www.computer.org

For industry information, contact the following organizations:

Software & Information Industry Association
1090 Vermont Avenue, NW, Sixth Floor
Washington, DC 20005-4095
Tel: 202-289-7442
http://www.siia.net

Software Testing Institute
http://www.softwaretestinginstitute.com

Software Engineers

QUICK FACTS

School Subjects
Computer science
Mathematics

Personal Skills
Mechanical/manipulative
Technical/scientific

Work Environment
Primarily indoors
Primarily one location

Minimum Education Level
Bachelor's degree

Salary Range
$49,350 to $79,780 to
$150,000+

Certification or Licensing
Recommended

Outlook
Much faster than the
average

DOT
030

GOE
02.07.01

NOC
2173

O*NET-SOC
15-1031.00, 15-1032.00

OVERVIEW

Software engineers are responsible for customizing existing software programs to meet the needs and desires of a particular business or industry. First, they spend considerable time researching, defining, and analyzing the problem at hand. Then, they develop software programs to resolve the problem on the computer. There are about 800,000 software engineers employed in the United States.

HISTORY

Advances in computer technology have enabled professionals to put computers to work in a range of activities once thought impossible. In the past several years, software engineers have been able to take advantage of computer hardware improvements in speed, memory capacity, reliability, and accuracy to create programs that do just about anything. Computer engineering blossomed as a distinct subfield in the computer industry after the new performance levels were achieved. This relative lateness is explained by the fact that the programs written by software engineers to solve business and scientific problems are very intricate and complex, requiring a lot of computing power. Although many computer scientists will continue to focus their research on further developing hardware, the emphasis in the field has moved to software, and the U.S. Department of Labor predicts that software engineers will be among the fastest-growing occupations in the United States through the next decade.

THE JOB

Every day, businesses, scientists, and government agencies encounter difficult problems that they cannot solve manually, either because the problem is just too complicated or because it would take too much time to calculate the appropriate solutions. For example, astronomers receive thousands of pieces of data every hour from probes and satellites in space as well as from telescopes here on Earth. If they had to process the information themselves, compile careful comparisons with previous years' readings, look for patterns or cycles, and keep accurate records of the origin of the data, it would be so cumbersome and lengthy a project as to make it next to impossible. They can, however, process the data with the extensive help of computers. Computer software engineers define and analyze specific problems in business or science and help develop computer software applications that effectively solve them. The software engineers who work in the field of astronomy are well versed in its concepts, but many other kinds of software engineers exist as well.

Software engineers fall into two basic categories. *Systems software engineers* build and maintain entire computer systems for a company. *Applications software engineers* design, create, and modify general computer applications software or specialized utility programs.

Engineers who work on computer systems research how a company's departments and their respective computer systems are organized. For example, there might be customer service, ordering, inventory, billing, shipping, and payroll recordkeeping departments. Systems software engineers suggest ways to coordinate all these parts. They might set up intranets or networks that link computers within the organization and ease communication.

Some applications software engineers develop packaged software applications, such as word processing, graphic design, or database programs, for software development companies. Other applications engineers design customized software for individual businesses or organizations. For example, a software engineer might work with an insurance company to develop new ways to reduce paperwork, such as claim forms, applications, and bill processing. Applications engineers write programs using programming languages like C++ and Java.

Software engineers sometimes specialize in a particular industry such as the chemical industry, insurance, or health care, which requires knowledge of that industry in addition to computer expertise. Some engineers work for consulting firms that complete software projects for different clients on an individual basis. Others work for large companies that hire full-time engineers to develop software customized to their needs.

Software engineering technicians assist engineers in completing projects. They are usually knowledgeable in analog, digital, and microprocessor electronics and programming techniques. Technicians know enough about program design and computer languages to fill in details left out by engineers or programmers, who conceive of the program from a large-scale perspective. Technicians might also test new software applications with special diagnostic equipment.

Both systems and applications software engineering involve extremely detail-oriented work. Since computers do only what they are programmed to do, engineers have to account for every bit of information with a programming command. Software engineers are thus required to be very well organized and precise. In order to achieve this, they generally follow strict procedures in completing an assignment.

First, they interview clients and colleagues to determine exactly what they want the final program to accomplish. Defining the problem by outlining the goal can sometimes be difficult, especially when clients have little technical training. Then, engineers evaluate the software applications already in use by the client to understand how and why they are failing to fulfill the needs of the operation. After this period of fact gathering, the engineers use methods of scientific analysis and mathematical models to develop possible solutions to the problems. These analytical methods help them predict and measure the outcomes of different proposed designs.

When they have developed a clear idea of what type of program is required to fulfill the client's needs, they draw up a detailed proposal that includes estimates of time and cost allocations. Management must then decide if the project will meet their needs, is a good investment, and whether or not it will be undertaken.

Once a proposal is accepted, both software engineers and technicians begin work on the project. They verify with hardware engineers that the proposed software program can be completed with existing hardware systems. Typically, the engineer writes program specifications and the technician uses his or her knowledge of computer languages to write preliminary programming. Engineers focus most of their effort on program strategies, testing procedures, and reviewing technicians' work.

Software engineers are usually responsible for a significant amount of technical writing, including project proposals, progress reports, and user manuals. They are required to meet regularly with clients to keep project goals clear and learn about any changes as quickly as possible.

When the program is completed, the software engineer organizes a demonstration of the final product to the client. Supervisors, management, and users are generally present. Some software engineers may offer to install the program, train users on it, and make arrangements for ongoing technical support.

REQUIREMENTS
High School
If you are interested in pursuing this career, take as many computer, math, and science courses as possible, because they provide fundamental math and computer knowledge and teach analytical thinking skills. Classes that rely on schematic drawing and flowcharts are also very valuable. English and speech courses will help you improve your communication skills, which are very important for software engineers.

Postsecondary Training
As more and more well-educated professionals enter the industry, most employers now require a bachelor's degree. A typical degree concentration for an applications software engineer is software engineering or computer science. Systems software engineers typically pursue a concentration in computer science or computer information systems.

Obtaining a postsecondary degree is usually considered challenging and even difficult. In addition to natural ability, you should be hard working and determined to succeed. If you plan to work in a specific technical field, such as medicine, law, or business, you should receive some formal training in that particular discipline.

Certification or Licensing
The Institute of Electrical and Electronics Engineers Computer Society offers the designation, certified software development professional, to individuals who have a bachelor's degree, a minimum of 9,000 hours of software engineering experience within at least six of 11 knowledge areas, and pass an examination. The Institute for Certification of Computing Professionals also offers basic certifications to computer professionals.

Another option if you're interested in software engineering is to pursue commercial certification. These programs are usually run by computer companies that wish to train professionals to work with their products. Classes are challenging and examinations can be rigorous. New programs are introduced every year.

Other Requirements
As a software engineer, you will need strong communications skills in order to be able to make formal business presentations and interact

with people having different levels of computer expertise. You must also be detail oriented and work well under pressure.

EXPLORING

Try to spend a day with a working software engineer or technician in order to experience firsthand what their job is like. School guidance counselors can help you arrange such a visit. You can also talk to your high school computer teacher for more information.

In general, you should be intent on learning as much as possible about computers and computer software. You should learn about new developments by reading trade magazines and talking to other computer users. You also can join computer clubs and surf the Internet for information about working in this field.

EMPLOYERS

About 800,000 computer software engineers are employed in the United States. Approximately 460,000 work with applications and 340,000 work with systems software. Software engineering is done in many fields, including medical, industrial, military, communications, aerospace, scientific, and other commercial businesses. Almost 30 percent of software engineers—the largest concentration in the field—work in computer systems design and related services.

STARTING OUT

If you have work experience and perhaps even an associate's degree, you may be promoted to a software engineering technician position from an entry-level job in quality assurance or technical support. Those already employed by computer companies or large corporations should read company job postings to learn about promotion opportunities. If you are already employed and would like to train in software engineering, either on the job or through formal education, you can investigate future career possibilities within your same company and advise management of your wish to change career tracks. Some companies offer tuition reimbursement for employees who train in areas applicable to business operations.

As a technical, vocational, or university student of software engineering, you should work closely with your school's career services offices, as many professionals find their first position through on-campus recruiting. Career services office staff are well trained to provide tips on resume writing, interviewing techniques, and locating job leads.

Individuals not working with a career services office can check the classified ads for job openings. They also can work with a local employment agency that places computer professionals in appropriate jobs. Many openings in the computer industry are publicized by word of mouth, so you should stay in touch with working computer professionals to learn who is hiring. In addition, these people may be willing to refer you directly to the person in charge of recruiting.

ADVANCEMENT

Software engineers who demonstrate leadership qualities and thorough technical know-how may become *project team leaders* who are responsible for full-scale software development projects. Project team leaders oversee the work of technicians and engineers. They determine the overall parameters of a project, calculate time schedules and financial budgets, divide the project into smaller tasks, and assign these tasks to engineers. Overall, they do both managerial and technical work.

Software engineers with experience as project team leaders may be promoted to a position as *software manager,* running a large research and development department. Managers oversee software projects with a more encompassing perspective; they help choose projects to be undertaken, select project team leaders and engineering teams, and assign individual projects. In some cases, they may be required to travel, solicit new business, and contribute to the general marketing strategy of the company.

Many computer professionals find that their interests change over time. As long as individuals are well qualified and keep up to date with the latest technology, they are usually able to find positions in other areas of the computer industry.

EARNINGS

Software engineers with a bachelor's degree in computer engineering earned starting salaries of $56,201 in 2007, according to the National Association of Colleges and Employers. Computer engineers specializing in applications earned median annual salaries of $79,780 in 2006, according to the U.S. Department of Labor. The lowest 10 percent averaged less than $49,350, and the highest 10 percent earned $119,770 or more annually. Software engineers specializing in systems software earned median salaries of $85,370 in 2006. The lowest paid 10 percent averaged $53,580 annually, and the highest paid engineers made $125,750 per year. Experienced software engineers can earn more than $150,000 a year. When software engineers are promoted to project team leader or software manager, they earn even more. Software engineers generally earn more in geographical areas where there are clusters of computer companies, such as the Silicon Valley in northern California.

Most software engineers work for companies that offer extensive benefits, including health insurance, sick leave, and paid vacation. In some smaller computer companies, however, benefits may be limited.

WORK ENVIRONMENT

Software engineers usually work in comfortable office environments. Overall, they usually work 40-hour weeks, but their hours depend on the nature of the employer and expertise of the engineer. In consulting firms, for example, it is typical for software engineers to work long hours and frequently travel to out-of-town assignments.

Software engineers generally receive an assignment and a time frame within which to accomplish it; daily work details are often left up to the individuals. Some engineers work relatively lightly at the beginning of a project, but work a lot of overtime at the end in order to catch up. Most engineers are not compensated for overtime. Software engineering can be stressful, especially when engineers must work to meet deadlines. Working with programming languages and intense details is often frustrating. Therefore, software engineers should be patient, enjoy problem-solving challenges, and work well under pressure.

OUTLOOK

The field of software engineering is expected to be one of the fastest growing occupations through 2014, according to the U.S. Department of Labor. Demands made on computers increase every day and from all industries. Rapid growth in the computer systems design and related industries will account for much of this growth. In addition, businesses will continue to implement new and innovative technology to remain competitive, and they will need software engineers to do this. Software engineers will also be needed to handle ever-growing capabilities of computer networks, e-commerce, and wireless technologies, as well as the security features needed to protect such systems from outside attacks. Outsourcing of jobs in this field to foreign countries will temper growth somewhat, but overall the future of software engineering is very bright.

Since technology changes so rapidly, software engineers are advised to keep up on the latest developments. While the need for software engineers will remain high, computer languages will probably change every few years and software engineers will need to attend seminars and workshops to learn new computer languages and software design. They also should read trade magazines, surf the Internet, and talk with colleagues about the field. These kinds of continuing education techniques help ensure that software engineers are best equipped to meet the needs of the workplace.

FOR MORE INFORMATION

For information on internships, student membership, and the student magazine Crossroads, *contact*
Association for Computing Machinery
2 Penn Plaza, Suite 701
New York, NY 10121-0701
Tel: 800-342-6626
Email: acmhelp@acm.org
http://www.acm.org

For certification information, contact
Institute for Certification of Computing Professionals
2350 East Devon Avenue, Suite 115
Des Plaines, IL 60018-4610
Tel: 800-843-8227
http://www.iccp.org

For information on career opportunities for women in computing, contact
Association for Women in Computing
41 Sutter Street, Suite 1006
San Francisco, CA 94104-5414
Tel: 415-905-4663
Email: info@awc-hq.org
http://www.awc-hq.org

For information on scholarships, certification, student membership, and to read Careers in Computer Science and Computer Engineering, *visit the IEEE's Web site:*
IEEE Computer Society
1730 Massachusetts Avenue, NW
Washington, DC 20036-1992
Tel: 202-371-0101
Email: membership@computer.org
http://www.computer.org

For more information on careers in computer software, contact
Software & Information Industry Association
1090 Vermont Avenue, NW, Sixth Floor
Washington, DC 20005-4095
Tel: 202-289-7442
http://www.siia.net

INTERVIEW

Dr. James McDonald is an associate professor and chair of the Department of Software Engineering at Monmouth University in West Long Branch, New Jersey. In addition to his experience as an educator, he has also worked at AT&T, Bell Laboratories, and Lucent Technologies. Dr. McDonald discussed the field with the editors of Careers in Focus: Computers.

Q. Please tell us about your program. What makes it stand out from other software engineering programs?

A. We offer a bachelor of science in software engineering (and also a master's degree). Our undergraduate program is one of only 15 undergraduate software engineering programs in the United States accredited by the Accreditation Board for Science and Engineering. [Visit http://www.monmouth.edu/academics/departments/software.asp to learn more.]

In addition to coursework in mathematics, science, and engineering our students also take a healthy dose of courses in business, social sciences, and the humanities, making them very well rounded and broadly educated by the time they complete their degree requirements. Virtually all of our students participate in one or more internships before they graduate.

Q. What is one thing that young people may not know about a career in software engineering?

A. Software engineering involves much more than purely technical work. Software engineers need to know how to work in large teams and interface with people well, both those that are similar to them and those that are very different.

Q. What types of students pursue study in your program?

A. Students with a wide variety of interests and abilities participate in our program. Those who do best, and are most successful in completing the program, are those who have done well in math and science courses in high school, are creative, and have a broad range of intellectual and interpersonal interests.

Q. What advice would you offer software engineering majors as they graduate and look for jobs?

A. Before they start looking they should have completed one or more internships in fields in which they think they might be interested in applying their software engineering skills and abilities. By *fields* I mean areas like pharmaceuticals, the aircraft industry, military applications, or telecommunications, all of which have significant needs for software engineering talent.

Q. What is the employment outlook for software engineers? What are the most promising employment segments in the field?

A. According to the U.S. Department of Labor, the need for software engineering talent will grow more rapidly between 2004 and 2014 than any other profession. It appears as though the greatest demands for talent are currently in the financial industry and in a variety of industries that support the U.S. Department of Defense.

Q. What is the future of your program?

A. Right now we are quite stable with approximately 50 students in our undergraduate program. We expect that the number of students will grow gradually over the next few years as it becomes obvious that industrial demand is growing. The structure of our program should not change much for the foreseeable future. But, as the program becomes larger, we will probably add elective courses that address the development of gaming software, information security, and computer forensics.

Systems Setup Specialists

QUICK FACTS

School Subjects
Business
Computer science

Personal Skills
Mechanical/manipulative
Technical/scientific

Work Environment
Primarily indoors
Primarily multiple locations

Minimum Education Level
High school diploma

Salary Range
$25,000 to $42,000 to
$100,000+

Certification or Licensing
Voluntary

Outlook
Faster than the average

DOT
030

GOE
02.06.01

NOC
2171

O*NET-SOC
15-1041.00

OVERVIEW

Systems setup specialists are responsible for installing new computer systems and upgrading existing ones to meet the specifications of the client. They install hardware, such as memory, sound cards, fax/modems, fans, microprocessors, and systems boards. They also load software and configure the hard drive appropriately. Some systems setup specialists install computer systems at the client's location. Installation might include normal hard drive or network server configurations as well as connecting peripherals such as printers, phones, fax machines, modems, and numerous terminals. They might also be involved with technical support in providing initial training to users. Systems setup specialists are employed by computer manufacturing companies or computer service companies nationwide, or may be employed as part of the technical support department of many businesses. Systems setup specialists are sometimes called *technical support technicians, desktop analyst/specialists,* and *PC setup specialists.*

HISTORY

Several big companies like IBM, Apple, Microsoft, and Intel have been the driving force behind various stages of the computer revolution. As technology advances, however, new companies spring up to compete with them. For example, IBM's first competitive challenge came when other companies decided to produce IBM-compatible PC clones. Today, the market for computers is saturated with different brands offering similar features. As a result, many companies are attempting

A freshman at Oregon State University solders the engine for a Tek Bot during her Electrical and Computer Orientation II class. *(Don Ryan, AP Images)*

to distinguish themselves from the competition by providing extra service to clients. Offering customized hardware and software is one way for them to do this. Systems setup specialists, therefore, are very important to sales. They ensure that clients receive exactly what they need and want. If the computer system is not set up correctly to begin with, clients might take their business elsewhere. As competition in the computer industry grows even fiercer, the customer service roles of systems setup specialists will become even more important.

THE JOB

Most businesses and organizations use computers on a daily basis. In fact, it is very difficult to find an office or store that does not use computer technology to help them with at least one business task. One thing is certain: There are so many different ways in which a business or individual can use computer technology that it would be impossible to count them. The wide variety could translate into big problems for computer companies if they tried to sell identical computer systems to every client. For example, a freelance writer would probably not be interested in a math card used for advanced mathematical calculations on personal computers. Likewise, a bank or insurance company has different database needs than a law firm.

In order to meet clients' various needs, many computer manufacturers, retailers, and service centers offer to customize commercial hardware and software for each client. Systems might differ by quantity of random access memory (RAM), speed and type of fax/modem, networking capabilities, and software packages. Systems setup specialists are responsible for installing new computer systems and upgrading existing ones to meet the specifications of the client. The main differences among setup specialists are their clients (individuals or businesses) and the level of systems they are qualified to work on.

Some specialists work in-house for large computer manufacturers, retailers, or service centers. Their clients are typically individuals buying for home use as well as small- to medium-sized businesses with minimal computing needs.

In the setup lab, specialists receive orders that list system specifications. Then, they follow instructions on how to set up the computer properly. They install hardware, such as memory chips, sound cards, fax/modems, fans, microprocessors, and system boards. They also install any software packages requested by the client. Next, they configure the hard drive so it knows exactly what hardware and software is connected to it. Finally, they run diagnostic tests on the system to make sure everything is running well.

The main goal is to eliminate the need for clients to do any setup work on the computer once they receive it. Clients should be able to plug it in, turn it on, and get it to work right away. In some cases, specialists even at this level will be sent to a client's location to install the system and provide some initial training on how to use it.

Other systems setup specialists work for companies that sell predominately to medium- and large-sized businesses. These specialists split their time between the employer's setup lab and the client's location. In the lab, they make initial preparations for installation. Some of the computer equipment might come from other manufacturers or suppliers, and so they have to verify that it is free of defects. They also check that they have all the necessary hardware parts, software packages, etc., before going to the client's location.

Depending on the size and complexity of the system to be installed, they might travel to the client's location one or more times before installation in order to map out the required wiring, communications lines, and space. It is very important to plan these details carefully. If wires are hard to reach, for example, future repairs and upgrade will be difficult. If the system is very large, setup specialists might recommend and build a raised floor in the client's computer center. The paneled floor allows easy access to the complex electrical and communications wiring.

Once thorough preparations have been made, setup specialists move the equipment to the clients' location to begin installation. Their on-site work might include configuring hard drives or network servers. They also connect peripherals: printers, phones, fax machines, modems, and numerous networked terminals. When everything is in place, they run extensive diagnostic tests in order to ensure that the system is running well. Invariably, they encounter problems. One terminal may not be able to send files to another, for example. Another terminal might be unable to establish fax communications outside the company. Solving problems requires consulting flow charts, other computer professionals, and technical manuals. The next round of testing occurs when the users begin working on the system. Some clients might prefer to simulate normal use while setup specialists stand by to correct problems. Large business installations can take days or even weeks to complete.

Sometimes, setup specialists are involved with technical support in training client users on the new system. They have to be well versed in the details of how to use the system properly and be able to explain it to individuals who might not know a lot about computers.

REQUIREMENTS
High School
If this industry interests you, try to take any mechanics and electronics classes that focus on understanding how complex machinery works. These classes will introduce you to the basics of reading flow charts and schematic drawings and understanding technical documents. The ability to read these documents efficiently and accurately is a prerequisite for computer setup work. Don't forget to take computer classes, especially those that explain the basic functioning of computer technology. English and speech classes will also help you build your communication skills, which is another important quality because setup specialists often work closely with many different people. Finally, take business classes to familiarize yourself with practices of the business world. These classes will also be of help to you if you decide to advance by starting your own business.

Postsecondary Training
A high school diploma is a minimum educational requirement for most systems setup specialist positions. However, the competitive nature of this industry is increasing the importance of postsecondary education, such as an associate's degree. Computer technology is advancing so rapidly that without a solid understanding of the basics, setup specialists cannot keep up with the changes. Also,

many aspiring computer professionals use system setup positions as a springboard to higher-level jobs in the company. Formal computer education, along with work experience, gives them a better chance for advancement.

Certification or Licensing

A number of companies, such as Microsoft and Cisco, offer certification programs in the use of their products. There are also independent companies that provide training programs leading to certification. Generally, these certifications are voluntary. Some employers may pay for part or all of the training cost.

Other Requirements

Do you work well with your hands? Manual work is performed on large and small scales. Sometimes thick cables and communications lines must be installed; other times tiny memory chips or microprocessors are needed. Therefore, you'll need to demonstrate good manual dexterity.

You should also be curious about how things work. Systems setup specialists are typically the kind of people who tinker around the house on DVD players, televisions, small appliances, and computers. Genuine curiosity of this type is important because you'll constantly be challenged to learn about new equipment and technologies. When things go wrong during installation, you will be called on to become an electronic and computer problem-solver and must be prepared with a solid understanding of the basics.

EXPLORING

There are several ways to obtain a better understanding of what it is like to be a setup specialist. One way is to try to organize a career day through school or friends and relatives. In this way, you could spend a day on the job with setup specialists and experience first-hand what the work entails.

You might also want to work part time for a computer repair shop. Repair shops usually do many upgrades that involve the installation of new hardware, like faster modems and microprocessors and more memory. Working in such a shop after school or on weekends will give you the opportunity to observe or practice the precision work of a setup specialist.

Depending on your level of computer knowledge, you may want to volunteer to setup new personal computers for friends or charitable organizations in your neighborhood. Try installing software or customizing some features of the operating system to better meet the needs of the user. To keep up to date on technology developments and get ideas for customizing, read computer magazines, such as *Computerworld* (http://www.computerworld.com) and *PC Magazine* (http://www.pcmag.com).

EMPLOYERS

In the early days of the computer industry, many jobs were clustered around northern California, where many of the big computer companies were headquartered. While good jobs are still available in this region, other top computer companies are located throughout the United States, and with them come a number of employment opportunities. Some computer hardware powerhouses include Dell, Hewlett-Packard, and IBM. Many mid- to small-sized companies may not have the need for a specific department devoted to computer setup. In such situations, other computer professionals may be assigned setup duties besides their regular job descriptions.

A number of jobs may also be found with smaller companies that contract their services to retail stores or offer them directly to the public. Services may include hardware and software installation, upgrading, and repair.

STARTING OUT

Most positions in systems setup are considered entry level. If you plan to enter this field without a postsecondary education but with computer skills and experience, you will need to network with working computer professionals for potential employment opportunities. Jobs are advertised in the newspaper every week; in fact, many papers devote entire sections to computer-related positions. Also, don't forget the benefits of working with employment agencies. Another job-hunting technique is to conduct online searches on the World Wide Web. Many computer companies post employment opportunities and accept resumes and applications online.

If you plan to enter the field by completing an advanced degree (in computer technology, for example), work closely with your school's career services office. Many firms looking for computer professionals inform schools first, since they are assured of meeting candidates with a certain level of proficiency in the field.

ADVANCEMENT

Within systems setup, there are several ways specialists can be promoted. One is by working on increasingly complex systems installations. Another is by having supervisory or managerial responsibility for the setup department. Other specialists choose to pursue promotion in different functional areas, such as technical support, computer engineering, or systems analysis.

When setup specialists demonstrate strong ability and drive, they are often assigned to larger and more complex installations. Instead of installing commercial software, for example, the specialist might now be responsible for constructing flow charts or other drawings as part of the overall installation plan. Also, a specialist who at first works on relatively small departmental networks might be asked to work on company-wide networks.

Computer professionals who use systems setup as a springboard to other positions usually have formal education in a certain field, such as software or hardware engineering. They seek promotion by keeping an eye on job openings within their respective fields.

If specialists show leadership ability, they might be promoted to supervisory and then managerial positions. These positions require more administrative duties and less hands-on work. For example, supervisors are usually in charge of scheduling installation jobs and assigning different jobs to various individuals, taking into account their level of expertise and experience. With more formal education, managers might be involved with the strategic planning of a computer company, deciding what level of service the company is willing to offer to clients.

Specialists may also decide to start their own computer business. Many office supply and electronic stores contract with area computer companies to provide customers with services such as setup and installation, upgrading, and technical support. Those who follow this career path should be familiar with the basics of operating a small business, such as doing accounting, marketing, and inventory.

EARNINGS

According to the 2006 Technical Support Salary Survey conducted by the Association of Support Professionals, systems setup specialists with entry-level customer service responsibilities earned $25,000 annually at the low end and had a median income of $35,000 annually; those working as support technicians had median annual earnings of $42,000. Senior support technicians, typically those with management responsibilities as well as experience and technical expertise, had a median annual salary of $55,000. In some areas of the country, salaries for those in management positions may be higher—ranging from $75,000 to $100,000 or more. Computer professionals typically earn more in areas where there are clusters of computer companies, such as in California and parts of the East Coast. However, the high cost of living in these areas may offset the benefits of a higher salary.

Most full-time setup specialists work for companies that provide a full range of benefits, including health insurance, sick leave, and paid vacation. In addition, many employers offer tuition reimbursement programs to employees who successfully complete course work in the field. Setup specialists who operate their own businesses are responsible for providing their own benefits.

WORK ENVIRONMENT

Systems setup specialists work primarily indoors, in a comfortable environment. This is not a desk job; specialists move around a lot either in the lab or at the client site. Travel to client locations is required for many setup specialists. The work also requires some lifting of heavy machinery, which can be avoided if an individual physically cannot perform this task. Given the nature of the work, dress is casual, although those who install systems at the client's site must be dressed in presentable business attire.

Setup specialists usually work a regular 40-hour week. However, they might be asked to work overtime when big installations are reaching final phases. They might have to work during off-hours if the client requires installation to be done then.

Installation work can be tedious. There are many details involving wiring, communications, and configurations. Setup specialists must therefore be patient and thorough, which can be frustrating at times. When problems arise, they must work well under stress and be able to think clearly about how to resolve the issues. If setup specialists are also involved in user training, they must communicate clearly and be understanding of others' problems.

OUTLOOK

Industry experts predict that demand for systems setup specialists will grow faster than the average for all other occupations. The U.S. Department of Labor reports that computer systems analysts, engineers, and scientists are expected to be among the fastest growing jobs through 2014. This outlook, however, may be somewhat tempered by the economic fluctuations in the technology industry as a whole. Nevertheless, the outlook remains good for systems setup specialists.

The ability to network and share information within the company allows businesses to be productive and work more efficiently. As new technology is developed, companies may upgrade or replace their systems altogether. Skilled workers will be in demand by companies to staff their technical support departments and provide services ranging from setup and installation to diagnostics.

Also, because of falling hardware and software prices, it has become more affordable for consumers to purchase home computers. Although advances in software technology have made program installation easy, computer companies will continue to offer installation services as a way to win customers from competitors. In addition, fierce competition will push companies to provide increasingly specialized service in terms of customization of computer systems. As computers become more sophisticated, highly trained setup specialists will be needed to install them correctly. It will therefore be very important for setup specialists to stay up to date with technological advances through continuing education, seminars, or work training.

FOR MORE INFORMATION

For information regarding the industry, career opportunities, and student membership, contact
Association for Computing Machinery
2 Penn Plaza, Suite 701
New York, NY 10121-0701
Tel: 800-342-6626
Email: acmhelp@acm.org
http://www.acm.org

For information regarding salary, employment opportunities nationwide, and industry news, contact
Association of Support Professionals
122 Barnard Avenue
Watertown, MA 02472-3414
Tel: 617-924-3944
http://www.asponline.com

For information on scholarships, student membership, and to read Careers in Computer Science and Computer Engineering, *visit the IEEE's Web site:*
IEEE Computer Society
1730 Massachusetts Avenue, NW
Washington, DC 20036-1992
Tel: 202-371-0101
Email: membership@computer.org
http://www.computer.org

Technical Writers and Editors

OVERVIEW

Technical writers, sometimes called *technical communicators*, express technical and scientific ideas in easy-to-understand language. *Technical editors* revise written text to correct any errors and make it read smoothly and clearly. They also may coordinate the activities of technical writers, technical illustrators, and other staff in preparing material for publication and oversee the document development and production processes. Technical writers hold about 45,000 jobs in the United States. Editors of all types (including technical editors) hold 127,000 jobs.

HISTORY

Humans have used writing to communicate information for over 5,500 years. Technical writing, though, did not emerge as a specific profession in the United States until the early years of the 20th century. Before that time, engineers, scientists, and researchers did any necessary writing themselves.

During the early 1900s, technology expanded rapidly. The use of machines to manufacture and mass-produce a wide number of products paved the way for more complex and technical products. Scientists and researchers were discovering new technologies and applications for technology, particularly in electronics, medicine, and engineering. The need to record studies and research, and report them to others, grew. Also, as products became more complex, it was necessary to provide information that documented their components, showed how they were assembled, and explained how to install, use, and repair them. By the mid-1920s, writers were being used to help engineers and scientists document their work and prepare technical information for nontechnical audiences.

Editors have worked with printers and authors for many years. They check copies of a printed document to correct any errors made during printing, to rewrite unclear passages, and to correct errors in spelling, grammar, and punctuation. As the need for technical writers grew, so too did the need for technical editors. Editors became more involved in documents before the printing stage, and today work closely with writers as they prepare their materials. Many editors coordinate the activities of all the people involved in preparing technical communications and manage the document development and production processes.

The need for technical writers grew further with the growth of the computer industry beginning in the 1960s. Originally, many computer companies used computer programmers to write user manuals and other documentation. It was widely assumed that the material was so complex that only those who were involved with creating computer programs would be able to write about them. Although computer programmers had the technical knowledge, many were not able to write clear, easy-to-use manuals. Complaints about the difficulty of using and understanding manuals were common. By the 1970s, computer companies began to hire technical writers to write computer manuals and documents. Today, this is one of the largest areas in which technical writers are employed.

The need for technical marketing writers also grew as a result of expanding computer technology. Many copywriters who worked for advertising agencies and marketing firms did not have the technical background to be able to describe the features of the technical products that were coming to market. Thus developed the need for writers who could combine the ability to promote products with the ability to communicate technical information.

The nature of technical writers' and technical editors' jobs continues to change with emerging technologies. Today, the ability to store, transmit, and receive information through computers and electronic means is changing the very nature of documents. Traditional books and paper documents are being replaced by CD-ROMs, interactive multimedia documents, and material accessed through bulletin board systems, faxes, the World Wide Web, and the Internet.

THE JOB

Technical writers and editors prepare a wide variety of documents and materials. The most common types of documents they produce are manuals, technical reports, specifications, and proposals. Some technical writers also write scripts for videos and audiovisual presentations and text for multimedia programs. Technical writers and editors prepare manuals that give instructions and detailed information on how to install, assemble, use, service, or repair a product or equipment. They may write and edit manuals as simple as a two-page leaflet that gives instructions on how to assemble a bicycle or as complex as a 500-page document that tells service technicians how to repair machinery, medical equipment, or a climate-control system. One of the most common types of manuals is the computer software manual, which informs users on how to load software on their computers, explains how to use the program, and gives information on different features.

Technical writers and editors also prepare technical reports on a multitude of subjects. These reports include documents that give the results of research and laboratory tests and documents that describe the progress of a project. They also write and edit sales proposals, product specifications, quality standards, journal articles, in-house style manuals, and newsletters.

The work of a technical writer begins when he or she is assigned to prepare a document. The writer meets with members of an account or technical team to learn the requirements for the document, the intended purpose or objectives, and the audience. During the planning stage, the writer learns when the document needs to be completed, approximately how long it should be, whether artwork or illustrations are to be included, who the other team members are, and any other production or printing requirements. A schedule is created that defines the different stages of development and determines when the writer needs to have certain parts of the document ready.

The next step in document development is the research, or information gathering, phase. During this stage, technical writers gather all the available information about the product or subject, read and review it, and determine what other information is needed. They may research the topic by reading technical publications, but in most cases they will need to gather information directly from the people working on the product. Writers meet with and interview people who are sources of information, such as scientists, engineers, software developers, computer programmers, managers, and project managers. They ask questions, listen, and take notes or record interviews. They gather any available notes, drawings, or diagrams that may be useful.

After writers gather all the necessary information, they sort it out and organize it. They plan how they are going to present the information and prepare an outline for the document. They may decide how the document will look and prepare the design, format, and layout of the pages. In some cases, this may be done by an editor rather than the writer. If illustrations, diagrams, or photographs are going to be included, either the editor or writer makes arrangements for an illustrator, photographer, or art researcher to produce or obtain them.

Then, the writer starts writing and prepares a rough draft of the document. If the document is very large, a writer may prepare it in segments. Once the rough draft is completed, it is submitted to a designated person or group for technical review. Copies of the draft are distributed to managers, engineers, or other experts who can easily determine if any technical information is inaccurate or missing. These reviewers read the document and suggest changes.

The rough draft is also given to technical editors for review of a variety of factors. The editors check that the material is organized well, that each section flows with the section before and after it, and that the language is appropriate for the intended audience. They also check for correct use of grammar, spelling, and punctuation. They ensure that names of parts or objects are consistent throughout the document and that references are accurate. They also check the labeling of graphs and captions for accuracy. Technical editors use special symbols, called proofreader's marks, to indicate the types of changes needed.

The editor and reviewers return their copies of the document to the technical writer. The writer incorporates the appropriate suggestions and revisions and prepares the final draft. The final draft is once again submitted to a designated reviewer or team of reviewers. In some cases, the technical reviewer may do a quick check to make sure that the requested changes were made. In other cases, the technical reviewer may examine the document in depth to ensure technical accuracy and correctness. A walkthrough, or test of the document, may be done for certain types of documents. For example, a walkthrough may be done for a document that explains how to assemble a product. A tester assembles the product by following the instructions given in the document. The tester makes a note of all sections that are unclear or inaccurate, and the document is returned to the writer for any necessary revisions.

Once the final draft has been approved, the document is submitted to the technical editor, who makes a comprehensive check of the document. In addition to checking that the language is clear and reads smoothly, the editor ensures that the table of contents matches the different sections or chapters of a document, all illustrations and diagrams are correctly placed, all captions are matched to the correct picture, consistent terminology is used, and correct references are used in the bibliography and text.

The editor returns the document to either the *writer* or a *word processor*, who makes any necessary corrections. This copy is then checked by a *proofreader*. The proofreader compares the final copy against the editor's marked-up copy and makes sure that all changes were made. The document is then prepared for printing. In some cases, the writer is responsible for preparing camera-ready copy or electronic files for printing purposes, and in other cases, a print production coordinator prepares all material to submit to a printer.

Some technical writers specialize in a specific type of material. *Technical marketing writers* create promotional and marketing materials for technological products. They may write the copy for an advertisement for a technical product, such as a computer workstation or software, or they may write press releases about the product. They also write sales literature, product flyers, Web pages, and multimedia presentations.

Other technical writers prepare scripts for videotapes and films about technical subjects. These writers, called *scriptwriters*, need to have an understanding of film and video production techniques.

Some technical writers and editors prepare articles for scientific, medical, computer, or engineering trade journals. These articles may report the results of research conducted by doctors, scientists, or engineers or report on technological advances in a particular field. Some technical writers and editors also develop textbooks. They may receive articles written by engineers or scientists and edit and revise them to make them more suitable for the intended audience.

Technical writers and editors may create documents for a variety of media. Electronic media, such as compact discs and online services, are increasingly being used in place of books and paper documents. Technical writers may create materials that are accessed through bulletin board systems and the Internet or create computer-based resources, such as help menus on computer programs. They also create interactive, multimedia documents that are distributed on compact discs. Some of these media require knowledge of special computer programs that allow material to be hyperlinked, or electronically cross-referenced.

REQUIREMENTS

High School

In high school, you should take composition, grammar, literature, creative writing, journalism, social studies, math, statistics, engineering, computer science, and as many science classes as possible. Business courses are also useful as they explain the organizational structure of companies and how they operate.

Postsecondary Training

Most employers prefer to hire technical writers and editors who have a bachelor's or advanced degree. Many technical editors graduate with degrees in the humanities, especially English or journalism. Technical writers typically need to have a strong foundation in engineering, computers, or science. Many technical writers graduate with a degree in engineering or science and take classes in technical writing.

Many different types of college programs are available that prepare people to become technical writers and editors. A growing number of colleges are offering degrees in technical writing. Schools without a technical writing program may offer degrees in journalism or English. Programs are offered through English, communications, and journalism departments. Classes vary based on the type of program. In general, classes for technical writers include a core curriculum in writing and classes in algebra, statistics, logic, science, engineering, and computer programming languages. Useful classes for editors include technical writing, project management, grammar, proofreading, copyediting, and print production.

Many technical writers and editors earn a master's degree. In these programs, they study technical writing in depth and may specialize in a certain area, such as scriptwriting, instructional design, or multimedia applications. In addition, many nondegree writing programs are offered to technical writers and editors to hone their skills. Offered as extension courses or continuing education courses, these programs include courses on indexing, editing medical materials, writing for trade journals, and other related subjects.

Technical writers, and occasionally technical editors, are often asked to present samples of their work. College students should build a portfolio during their college years in which they collect their best samples from work that they may have done for a literary magazine, newsletter, or yearbook.

Technical writers and editors should be willing to pursue learning throughout their careers. As technology changes, technical writers and editors may need to take classes to update their knowledge. Changes in electronic printing and computer technology will also change the way technical writers and editors do their jobs, and writers and editors may need to take courses to learn new skills or new technologies.

Other Requirements

Technical writers need to have good communications skills, science and technical aptitudes, and the ability to think analytically. Technical editors also need to have good communications skills, and judgment, as well as the ability to identify and correct errors in written material. They need to be diplomatic, assertive, and able to explain tactfully what needs to be corrected to writers, engineers, and other people involved with a document. Technical editors should be able to understand technical information easily, but they need less scientific and technical background than writers. Both technical writers and editors need to be able to work as part of a team and collaborate with others on a project. They need to be highly self-motivated, well organized, and able to work under pressure.

EXPLORING

If you enjoy writing and are considering a career in technical writing or editing, you should make writing a daily activity. Writing is a skill that develops over time and through practice. You can keep journals, join writing clubs, and practice different types of writing, such as scriptwriting and informative reports. Sharing writing with others and asking them to critique it is especially helpful. Comments from readers on what they enjoyed about a piece of writing or difficulty they had in understanding certain sections provides valuable feedback that helps to improve your writing style.

Reading a variety of materials is also helpful. Reading exposes you to both good and bad writing styles and techniques and helps you identify why one approach works better than another.

You may also gain experience by working on a literary magazine, student newspaper, or yearbook (or starting one of your own if one is not available). Both writing and editing articles and managing production give you the opportunity to learn new skills and to see what is involved in preparing documents and other materials.

You may also be able to get internships, cooperative education assignments, or summer or part-time jobs as proofreaders or editorial assistants that may include writing responsibilities.

EMPLOYERS

There are approximately 45,000 technical writers currently employed in the United States. Editors of all types (including technical editors) hold 127,000 jobs.

Employment may be found in many different types of places, such as in the fields of aerospace, computers, engineering, pharmaceuticals, and research and development, or with the nuclear industry, medical publishers, government agencies or contractors, and colleges and universities. The aerospace, engineering, medical, and computer industries hire significant numbers of technical writers and editors. The federal government, particularly the Departments of Defense and Agriculture, the National Aeronautics and Space Administration, and the Nuclear Regulatory Commission, also hires many writers and editors with technical knowledge.

STARTING OUT

Many technical writers start their careers as scientists, engineers, technicians, or research assistants and move into writing after several years of experience in those positions. Technical writers with a bachelor's degree in a technical subject such as engineering may be able to find work as a technical writer immediately upon graduating from college, but many employers prefer to hire writers with some work experience.

Technical editors who graduate with a bachelor's degree in English or journalism may find entry-level work as *editorial assistants*, *copy editors*, or *proofreaders*. From these positions they are able to move into technical editing positions. Or beginning workers may find jobs as technical editors in small companies or those with a small technical communications department.

If you plan to work for the federal government, you need to pass an examination. Information about examinations and job openings is available at federal employment centers.

You may learn about job openings through your college's career services office and want ads in newspapers and professional magazines. You may also research companies that hire technical writers and editors and apply directly to them. Many libraries provide useful job resource guides and directories that provide information about companies that hire in specific areas.

ADVANCEMENT

As technical writers and editors gain experience, they move into more challenging and responsible positions. At first, they may work on simple documents or are assigned to work on sections of a document. As they demonstrate their proficiency and skills, they are given more complex assignments and are responsible for more activities.

Technical writers and editors with several years of experience may move into project management positions. As project managers, they are responsible for the entire document development and production processes. They schedule and budget resources and assign writers, editors, illustrators, and other workers to a project. They monitor the schedule, supervise workers, and ensure that costs remain in budget.

Technical writers and editors who show good project management skills, leadership abilities, and good interpersonal skills may become supervisors or managers. Both technical writers and editors can move into senior writer and senior editor positions. These positions involve increased responsibilities and may include supervising other workers.

Many technical writers and editors seek to develop and perfect their skills rather than move into management or supervisory positions. As they gain a reputation for their quality of work, they may be able to select choice assignments. They may learn new skills as a means of being able to work in new areas. For example, a technical writer may learn a new desktop program in order to become more proficient in designing. Or a technical writer may learn a hypermedia or hypertext computer program in order to be able to create a multimedia program. Technical writers and editors who broaden their skill base and capabilities can move to higher-paying positions within their own company or at another company. They also may work as freelancers or set up their own communications companies.

EARNINGS

Median annual earnings for salaried technical writers were $58,050 in 2006, according to the U.S. Department of Labor. Salaries ranged from less than $35,520 to more than $91,720. Editors of all types earned a median salary of $46,990 in 2006. The lowest-paid 10 percent earned $27,340 or less and the highest-paid 10 percent earned $87,400 or more.

Most companies offer benefits that include paid holidays and vacations, medical insurance, and 401(k) plans. They may also offer profit sharing, pension plans, and tuition assistance programs.

WORK ENVIRONMENT

Technical writers and editors usually work in an office environment, with well-lit and quiet surroundings. They may have their own offices or share work space with other writers and editors. Most writers and editors have computers. They may be able to utilize the services of support staff who can word-process revisions, run off copies, fax material, and perform other administrative functions or they may have to perform all of these tasks themselves.

Some technical writers and editors work out of home offices and use computer modems and networks to send and receive materials electronically. They may go into the office only on occasion for meetings and gathering information. Freelancers and contract workers may work at a company's premises or at home.

Although the standard workweek is 40 hours, many technical writers and editors frequently work 50 or 60 hours a week. Job interruptions, meetings, and conferences can prevent writers from having long periods of time to write. Therefore, many writers work after hours or bring work home. Both writers and editors frequently work in the evening or on weekends in order to meet a deadline.

In many companies there is pressure to produce documents as quickly as possible. Both technical writers and editors may feel at times that they are compromising the quality of their work due to the need to conform to time and budget constraints. In some companies, technical writers and editors may have increased workloads due to company reorganizations or downsizing. They may need to do the work that was formerly done by more than one person. Technical writers and editors also are increasingly assuming roles and responsibilities formerly performed by other people and this can increase work pressures and stress.

Despite these pressures, most technical writers and editors gain immense satisfaction from their work and the roles that they perform in producing technical communications.

OUTLOOK

The writing and editing field is generally very competitive. Each year, there are more people trying to enter this field than there are available openings. The field of technical writing and editing, though, offers more opportunities than other areas of writing and editing, such as book publishing or journalism. Employment opportunities for technical writers and editors are expected to grow about as fast as the average for all occupations through 2014. Demand is growing for technical writers who can produce well-written computer manuals. In addition to the computer industry, the pharmaceutical industry is showing an increased need for technical writers. Rapid growth in the high technology and electronics industries and the Internet will create a continuing demand for people to write users' guides, instruction manuals, and training materials. Technical writers will be needed to produce copy that describes developments and discoveries in law, science, and technology for a more general audience.

Writers may find positions that include duties in addition to writing. A growing trend is for companies to use writers to run a department, supervise other writers, and manage freelance writers and outside contractors. In addition, many writers are acquiring responsibilities that include desktop publishing and print production coordination.

The demand for technical writers and editors is significantly affected by the economy. During recessionary times, technical writers and editors are often among the first to be laid off. Many companies today are continuing to downsize or reduce their number of employees and are reluctant to keep writers on staff. Such companies prefer to hire writers and editors on a temporary contractual basis, using them only as long as it takes to complete an assigned document. Technical writers and editors who work on a temporary or freelance basis need to market their services and continually look for new assignments. They also do not have the security or benefits offered by full-time employment.

FOR MORE INFORMATION

For information on writing and editing careers in the field of communications, contact
National Association of Science Writers
PO Box 890
Hedgesville, WV 25427-0890
Tel: 304-754-5077
http://www.nasw.org

For information on careers, contact
Society for Technical Communication
901 North Stuart Street, Suite 904
Arlington, VA 22203-1822
Tel: 703-522-4114
Email: stc@stc.org
http://www.stc.org

Webmasters

OVERVIEW

Webmasters design, implement, and maintain Internet Web sites for corporations, educational institutions, not-for-profit organizations, government agencies, or other institutions. Webmasters should have working knowledge of network configurations, interface, graphic design, software development, business, writing, marketing, and project management. Because the function of a webmaster encompasses so many different responsibilities, the position is often held by a team of individuals in a large organization.

HISTORY

The Internet developed from ARPANET, an experimental computer network established in the 1960s by the U.S. Department of Defense. By the late 1980s, the Internet was being used by many government and educational institutions.

The World Wide Web was the brainchild of physicist Tim Berners-Lee. Although Berners-Lee formed his idea of the Web in 1989, it was another four years before the first Web browser (Mosaic) made it possible to navigate the Web simply. Businesses quickly realized the commercial potential of the Web and soon developed their own Web sites.

No one person or organization is in charge of the Internet and what's on it. However, each Web site needs an individual, or team of workers, to gather, organize, and maintain online data. These specialists, called webmasters, manage sites for businesses of all sizes, nonprofit organizations, schools, government agencies, and private individuals.

THE JOB

Because the idea of designing and maintaining a Web site is relatively new, there is no complete, definitive job description for webmasters. Many of their job responsibilities depend on the goals and needs of the particular organization for which they work. There are, however, some basic duties common to almost all webmasters.

Webmasters, specifically site managers, first secure space on the Web for the site they are developing. This is done by contracting with an Internet service provider. The provider serves as a sort of storage facility for the organization's online information, usually charging a set monthly fee for a specified amount of megabyte space. The webmaster may also be responsible for establishing a uniform resource locator, or URL, for the Web site he or she is developing. The URL serves as the site's online "address" and must be registered with InterNIC, the Web URL registration service.

The webmaster is responsible for developing the actual Web site for his or her organization. In some cases, this may involve actually writing the text content of the pages. More commonly, however, the webmaster is given the text to be used and is merely responsible for programming it in such a way that it can be displayed on a Web page. In larger companies, webmasters specialize in content, adaptation, and presentation of data.

In order for text to be displayed on a Web page, it must be formatted using hypertext markup language (HTML). HTML is a system of coding text so that the computer that is "reading" it knows how to display it. For example, text could be coded to be a certain size or color or to be italicized or boldface. Paragraphs, line breaks, alignment, and margins are other examples of text attributes that must be coded in HTML.

Although it is less and less common, some webmasters code text manually, by actually typing the various commands into the body of the text. This method is time consuming, however, and mistakes are easily made. More often, webmasters use a software program that automatically codes text. Some word processing programs, such as WordPerfect, even offer HTML options.

Along with coding the text, the webmaster must lay out the elements of the Web site in such a way that it is visually pleasing, well organized, and easy to navigate. He or she may use various colors, background patterns, images, tables, or charts. These graphic elements can come from image files already on the Web, software clip art files, or images scanned into the computer with an electronic scanner. In some cases, when an organization is using the Web site to promote its product or service, the webmaster may work with a marketing specialist or department to develop a page.

Some Web sites have several directories or "layers." That is, an organization may have several Web pages, organized in a sort of "tree," with its home page connected, via hypertext links, to other pages, which may in turn be linked to other pages. The webmaster is responsible for organizing the pages in such a way that a visitor can easily browse through them and find what he or she is looking for. Such webmasters are called programmers and developers; they are also responsible for creating Web tools and special Web functionality.

For webmasters who work for organizations that have several different Web sites, one responsibility may be making sure that the "style" or appearance of all the pages is the same. This is often referred to as "house style." In large organizations, such as universities, where many different departments may be developing and maintaining their own pages, it is especially important that the webmaster monitor these pages to ensure consistency and conformity to the organization's requirements. In almost every case, the webmaster has the final authority for the content and appearance of his or her organization's Web site. He or she must carefully edit, proofread, and check the appearance of every page.

Besides designing and setting up Web sites, most webmasters are charged with maintaining and updating existing sites. Most sites contain information that changes regularly. Some change daily or even hourly. Depending on his or her employer and the type of Web site, the webmaster may spend a good deal of time

How Many People Are Online?

Asia/Pacific:	436,758,162
Europe:	321,853,477
North America:	232,655,287
South America:	77,978,800
Africa:	33,545,600
Central America:	25,997,600
Middle East:	19,539,300
Oceania:	18,796,490

Source: Internet World Stats, June 2007

updating and remodeling the page. He or she is also responsible for ensuring that the hyperlinks contained within the Web site lead to the sites they should. Since it is common for links to change or become obsolete, the webmaster usually performs a link check every few weeks.

Other job duties vary, depending on the employer and the position. Most webmasters are responsible for receiving and answering email messages from visitors to the organization's Web site. Some webmasters keep logs and create reports on when and how often their pages are visited and by whom. Depending on the company, Web sites count anywhere from 300 to 1.4 billion visits, or "hits," a month. Some create and maintain order forms or online "shopping carts" that allow visitors to the Web site to purchase products or services. Some may train other employees on how to create or update Web pages. Finally, webmasters may be responsible for developing and adhering to a budget for their departments.

REQUIREMENTS

High School

High school students who are interested in becoming webmasters should take as many computer science classes as they can. Mathematics classes are also helpful. Finally, because writing skills are important in this career, English classes are good choices.

Postsecondary Training

A number of community colleges, colleges, and universities offer classes and certificate programs for webmasters, but there is no standard educational path or requirement for becoming a webmaster. While many have bachelor's degrees in computer science, information systems, or computer programming, liberal arts degrees, such as English, are not uncommon. There are also webmasters who have degrees in engineering, mathematics, and marketing.

Certification or Licensing

There is strong debate within the industry regarding certification. Some, mostly corporate chief executive officers, favor certification. They view certification as a way to gauge an employee's skill and expertise. Others argue, however, that it is nearly impossible to test knowledge of technology that is constantly changing and improving. Despite the split of opinion, webmaster certification programs are available at many colleges, universities, and technical schools throughout the United States. Programs vary in length, anywhere from three weeks to nine months or more. Topics covered include client/server technology, Web development, programs, and software and hardware. The International Webmasters Association and World Organization of Webmasters also offer voluntary certification programs.

Should webmasters be certified? Though it's currently not a prerequisite for employment, certification can only enhance a candidate's chance at landing a webmaster position.

What most webmasters have in common is a strong knowledge of computer technology. Most people who enter this field are already well versed in computer operating systems, programming languages, computer graphics, and Internet standards. When considering candidates for the position of webmaster, employers usually require at least two years of experience with World Wide Web technologies. In some cases, employers require that candidates already have experience in designing and maintaining Web sites. It is, in fact, most common for someone to move into the position of webmaster from another computer-related job in the same organization.

Other Requirements
Webmasters should be creative. It is important for a Web page to be designed well in order to attract attention. Good writing skills and an aptitude for marketing are also excellent qualities for anyone considering a career in Web site design.

EXPLORING

One of the easiest ways to learn about what a webmaster does is to spend time surfing the World Wide Web. By examining a variety of Web sites to see how they look and operate, you can begin to get a feel for what goes into a home page.

Growth in Number of Web Sites

September 1993	204
August 1996	342,081
August 2000	19,823,296
August 2005	70,392,567
August 2006	96,854,877

Source: Hobbes Internet Timeline

An even better way to explore this career is to design your own personal Web page. Many Internet servers offer their users the option of designing and maintaining a personal Web page for a very low fee. A personal page can contain virtually anything that you want to include, from snapshots of friends to audio files of favorite music to hypertext links to other favorite sites.

EMPLOYERS

The majority of webmasters working today are full-time employees, according to *Interactive Week*. They are employed by Web design companies, businesses, schools or universities, not-for-profit organizations, government agencies—in short, any organization that requires a presence on the World Wide Web. Webmasters may also work as freelancers or operate their own Web design businesses.

STARTING OUT

Most people become webmasters by moving into the position from another computer-related position within the same company. Since most large organizations already use computers for various functions, they may employ a person or several people to serve as computer "specialists." If these organizations decide to develop their own Web sites, they frequently assign the task to an employee already experienced with the computer system. Often, the person who ultimately becomes an organization's webmaster at first just takes on the job in addition to his or her other, already established duties.

Another way that individuals find jobs in this field is through online postings of job openings. Many companies post webmaster position openings online because the candidates they hope to attract are very likely to use the Internet for a job search. Therefore, the prospective webmaster should use the World Wide Web to check job-related newsgroups. He or she might also use a Web search engine to locate openings.

ADVANCEMENT

Experienced webmasters employed by a large organization may be able to advance to the position of *chief Web officer*. Chief Web officers supervise a team of webmasters and are responsible for every aspect of a company's presence on the Web. Others might advance by starting their own business, designing Web sites on a contractual basis for several clients rather than working exclusively for one organization.

Opportunities for webmasters of the future are endless due to the continuing development of online technology. As understanding and use of the World Wide Web increase, there may be new or expanded job duties in the future for individuals with expertise in this field.

EARNINGS

The average salary for webmasters in 2007 was $66,975, according to Salary.com. Salaries ranged from less than $45,427 to more than $91,031. However, many webmasters move into the position from another position within their company or have taken on the task in addition to other duties. These employees are often paid approximately the same salary they were already making.

According to the National Association of Colleges and Employers, the starting salary for graduates with a bachelor's degree in computer science was $51,070 in 2006. Those with a bachelor's degree in information sciences and systems had average starting salary offers of $47,182.

Depending on the organization for which they work, webmasters may receive a benefits package in addition to salary. A typical benefits package would include paid vacations and holidays, medical insurance, and perhaps a pension plan.

WORK ENVIRONMENT

Although much of the webmaster's day may be spent alone, it is nonetheless important that he or she be able to communicate and work well with others. Depending on the organization for which he or she works, the webmaster may meet periodically with graphic designers, marketing specialists, writers, or other professionals who have input into Web site development. In many larger organizations, there is a team of webmasters rather than just one. Although each team member works alone on his or her own specific duties, the members may meet frequently to discuss and coordinate their activities.

Because technology changes so rapidly, this job is constantly evolving. Webmasters must spend time reading and learning about new developments in online communication. They may be continually working with new computer software or hardware. Their actual job responsibilities may even change, as the capabilities of both the organization and the World Wide Web itself expand. It is important that these employees be flexible and willing to learn and grow with the technology that drives their work.

Because they don't deal with the general public, most webmasters are allowed to wear fairly casual attire and to work in a relaxed atmosphere. In most cases, the job calls for standard working hours, although there may be times when overtime is required.

OUTLOOK

According to the U.S. Department of Labor, the field of computer and data processing services is projected to be among the fastest growing industries for the next decade. As a result, the employment rate of webmasters and other computer specialists is expected to grow much faster than the average for all occupations through 2014.

There can be no doubt that computer, and specifically online, technology will continue its rapid growth for the next several years. Likewise, then, the number of computer-related jobs, including that of webmaster, should also increase. As more and more businesses, not-for-profit organizations, educational institutions, and government agencies choose to "go online," the total number of Web sites will grow, as will the need for experts to design them. Growth will be largest for Internet content developers (webmasters responsible for the information displayed on a Web site) and chief Web officers.

One thing to keep in mind, however, is that when technology advances extremely rapidly, it tends to make old methods of doing things obsolete. If current trends continue, the responsibilities of the webmaster will be carried out by a group or department instead of a single employee, in order to keep up with the demands of the position. It is possible that in the next few years, changes in technology will make Web sites as we know them today things of the past. Another possibility is that, like desktop publishing, user-friendly software programs will make Web site design so easy and efficient that it no longer requires an "expert" to do it well. Webmasters who are concerned with job security should be willing to continue learning and using the very latest developments in technology, so that they are prepared to move into the future of online communication, whatever it may be.

FOR MORE INFORMATION

For information on training and certification programs, contact the following organizations:

International Webmasters Association
119 East Union Street, Suite F
Pasadena, CA 91103-3952
Tel: 626-449-3709
http://www.iwanet.org

World Organization of Webmasters
PO Box 1743
Folsom, CA 95630-1743
Tel: 916-989-2933
Email: info@joinwow.org
http://www.joinwow.org

Index